THE COLLECTOR OF
POSITIVE COMPONENTS
A LAW OF ATTRACTION TOOL

By
Awaken Within Law Of Attraction Tools
Copyright © 2018

More by the author

Law of Attraction 31-day Interactive Workbook All subjects
A 31-day interactive workbook that covers all subjects. Designed to shift your
thinking and vibration strongly over the course of the month. Contains
exciting storylines which are given to you from your Inner Being. Interactive,
so it won't have to be printed and can be carried with you everywhere.
It can be used on any device with a pdf reading program.
Instant delivery using trusted digital download service SendOwl and Paypal,
which are safe & secure.
For sale through:
Facebook Awaken Within: Law Of Attraction Tools

Facebook group:
/www.facebook.com/groups/AbrahamHicksThoughtstoThings

MY
30 DAY CHALLENGE

STARTING DATE:_____

Everything is vibrationally achieved. You must take the emotional Journey.

Law of Attraction responds to the energy you express in the moments that make up your day.

The hindering of all outcomes happens when you are expressing energy by focusing on where the creation is during the process of the manifestation.

This just recreates the same place moment by moment.

Place daily focus on finding a feeling that creates a content and satisfied feeling.

This is an ongoing process all day.

It may feel mechanical but that will soon go away as you become more used to holding and focusing on these new pleasing feelings. This happens until you build enough momentum behind this rehearsed action.

Life is supposed to be fun.

If you are not enjoying yourself you are focused too strongly on a subject. Soften your focus, pull back and go general.

 MY 30 Day

STORY

The benefits of imagination are powerful. There is no difference to the universe what you are using to focus on and express emotions with.

As I read my ideal story each day, I will reach for the feelings of how good this story feels to me. I don't care if it is true or not, I am using it to create my feel-good vibrations that create my future manifestations.

_____
_____
_____
_____
_____
_____
_____
_____
_____
_____
_____
_____
_____
_____
_____
_____
                                    _____

1 SIT FOR ONE MINUTE BREATHING

Focus on holding a smile while taking in long and deep breaths in and slowly letting them out. Relax your body and feel the comfort of where you sit.

2 REMIND YOURSELF HOW IMPORTANT IT IS TO FEEL GOOD.

Today, nothing is more important then I feel good.

3

Write that here:

_____
_____
_____
_____
_____
_____

5

NOTICE HOW THE SUN CAME UP AND THINGS ARE ALWAYS IN MOTION.

4

Close your eyes and see yourself aligning with source, blending into one.
Thank this constant focus upon you.

6

Feel and give thanks for the abundance of well-being all around.
For a full minute.

What 4 things would I like to turn over to the Universe to take care of for me today?

1._____
2._____
3._____
4._____

When you stop looking for the desired manifestation, you learn that the feeling grows and carries you to the destination.

Write what things you intend to do today and how you intend to feel as you accomplish these things.

1._____Feeling_____
2._____Feeling_____
3._____Feeling_____
4._____Feeling_____

I look forward to enjoying a productive and fun day.

Pick one of these emotions you would like to use
as today's intended feeling.
Ease, Relaxed, Comfort
Write this feeling here:_____
Now say to yourself...

1.
MY INTENTION IS TO REMIND MYSELF MANY TIMES TODAY...

FOCUSING ON THIS FEELING OF_____ IS MY REAL JOB FOR THE DAY.

2.
MY CURRENT CONDITIONS ARE IRRELEVANT BECAUSE...

I'M CREATING AN ENVIRONMENT THAT IS CAUSING THEM TO CHANGE.

3.
NO MORE SNAPSHOTS OF WHAT IS OR FEELING HELPLESS.

TODAY, I AM GOING TO USE THIS EMOTION AS MY BASE FEELING THAT WILL EFFECT FUTURE OUTCOMES.

Close your eyes again and reach for this intended feeing in place of the feeling of current reality. Notice the softening of your body as you aligning with source.

Write your chosen daily focused emotion reaching for the feeling.

_____ _____ _____
_____ _____ _____
_____ _____ _____
_____ _____ _____

ASK YOURSELF MANY TIMES TODAY
"Is this the attracting vibration, I want the universe to respond to?"
If not, for the count of 10 long breaths in and
slowly letting them out.
Say and feel your chosen emotion in appreciation for the feeling.
It self-creates without any evidence needed.

Write 3 things you would be interested in seeing that just for fun but you are not worried about when.

_____
_____
_____

Let the universe show you these things in playful and exciting ways.

A THOUGHT REACHES A COMBUSTION POINT AT 16 SECONDS.

VIBRATIONAL CASH

A FULL 68 SECONDS ARE EQUIVALENT TO 2 MILLION MAN-HOURS.

Spend Your Vibrational Cash on one thing a day. If wanting a big ticket item slowly pay it off. This will make it more real for you.

The longer you spend feeling like the recipient of this desire the closer you are in being a match to it.

Focus on how it feels to buy this desire and the satisfaction attached within having it. Write about that satisfaction.

Close your eyes again and reach for the first thing that pops into your mind. No matter what the price tag is, big and small creations are all the same. Learn to start treating them all equal.

VIBRATIONALCASH

DATE _____

PAY TO THE ORDER OF

5,000.00

IN YOUR CURRENCY

LIVE THE EXPERIENCE IN THE NOW

FOR _____

SIGN NAME HERE

_____

_____

_____

_____

_____

_____

_____

_____

_____

ASK, BELIEVE, RECEIVE

ASK

What are ready to take the vibrational journey to?
By asking for this desire it means you are creating a gap and your job is to close it.

BELIEVE/SOURCE

THE MINUTE YOU ASK, IT IS DONE VIBRATIONALLY COMPLETE AND 99.99% DONE PHYSICALLY

RECEIVE:

Create a momentum in belief by feeling it is yours for 20 second, snap shots at a time. Focusing only on feeling not image.

If you hold an emotion as the desire. You no longer are creating an impossibility. The shift from in the future having the desire becomes felt in the present moment, and you will notice the tension has left the solar plexus as you do this.
At this moment you are able to isolate the components of the desire even without having the desire. You become expectant, Being expectant is a very high frequency, and it is one step away from the manifestation to occur.

What do you feel ready to change in your life.
By asking you are now saying "I will deliberately start creating this climate to close the gap.
I am aware of my part in how long the manifestation will take.

_____

_____

_____

_____

_____

Source has now become this vibrationally.
Your work is to create a mimicking or matching vibration.

Faith is created by reaching for the feeling and trusting the manifestation will follow.
Start now creating the feeling it is done by using small 20-second Virtual Realities while conjuring the emotions.
The idea is to preserve the focus that feels good longer, so you can match the frequency and enjoy the pleasures it provides in feelings.
Always leave the imagination play through, if you feel anything but enjoyment.

POSITIVE ASPECTS

Appreciation is one of the highest vibrations you can use to shift how you are feeling.
It will build momentum fast and create an overall positive experience.
Even when you are in the worst of moods, if you focus on the parts that
you are appreciative for you will begin to start a new point of attraction.

I APPRECIATE YOU!
PERSON
NAME: *WHY?*

_____
_____
_____
_____
_____

I APPRECIATE THE
BEAUTY FOUND HERE.
PLACE: *WHY?*

_____
_____
_____
_____
_____

I APPRECIATE THE
BEAUTY FOUND HERE.
PLACE: *WHY?*

_____
_____
_____
_____
_____

I APPRECIATE YOU!
PERSON   *WHY?*
NAME:

_____
_____
_____
_____

I APPRECIATE HAVING
ACCESS TO THIS.
THING: *WHY?*

_____
_____
_____
_____

WHAT I LOVE ABOUT
THE WEATHER: *WHY?*

_____
_____
_____
_____

I APPRECIATE YOU!
PERSON
NAME: *WHY?*

_____
_____
_____
_____

I APPRECIATE HAVING
ACCESS TO THIS.
THING: *WHY?*

_____
_____
_____
_____

WHAT I LOVE ABOUT..

WHY?

_____
_____
_____
_____

POSITIVE
ASPECTS

Focus on anything and everything. Saying "thank you"
Creates more things to be thankful for.

I AM THANKFUL FOR: *WHY?*

_____
_____
_____
_____
_____

I AM THANKFUL FOR: *WHY?*

_____
_____
_____
_____
_____

I AM THANKFUL FOR: *WHY?*

_____
_____
_____
_____
_____

I AM THANKFUL FOR: *WHY?*

_____
_____
_____
_____
_____

I AM THANKFUL FOR: *WHY?*

_____
_____
_____
_____
_____

I AM THANKFUL FOR: *WHY?*

_____
_____
_____
_____
_____

I AM THANKFUL FOR: *WHY?*

_____
_____
_____
_____
_____

I AM THANKFUL FOR: *WHY?*

_____
_____
_____
_____
_____

I AM THANKFUL FOR: *WHY?*

_____
_____
_____
_____
_____

FOODS

yum! WHAT MY BODY ENJOYED TODAY

_____
_____
_____
_____
_____
_____

WATER INTAKE

AM I HYDRATED?

GET PHYSICAL

WHAT MOVEMENT DID MY BODY ENJOY TODAY

_____
_____
_____
_____

MEDITATION

SPEND 15 MINS FOCUSING ON REPETITIVE SOUND. THE MORE BORING IT IS THE BETTER.

A TO Z

WRITE WORDS FROM A TO Z FEELING FOR THEM AS YOU WRITE THEM MAKE UP WORDS IF YOU CANT THINK OF ONE.

A_____ B_____ C_____ D_____

E_____ F_____ G_____ H_____

I_____ J_____ K_____ L_____

M_____ N_____ O_____ P_____

Q_____ R_____ S_____ T_____

U_____ V_____ W_____ X_____

Y_____ Z_____

Am I match ____
If I am feeling ease and comfort in this moment then I am.
I will sit in the feeling of satisfaction at focusing on these emotions right now.

1 SIT FOR ONE MINUTE BREATHING

Focus on holding a smile while taking in long and deep breaths in and slowly letting them out. Relax your body and feel the comfort of where you sit.

2 REMIND YOURSELF HOW IMPORTANT IT IS TO FEEL GOOD.

Today, nothing is more important then I feel good.

3

Write that here:

_____
_____
_____
_____
_____
_____
_____

5

NOTICE HOW THE SUN CAME UP AND THINGS ARE ALWAYS IN MOTION.

4

Close your eyes and see yourself aligning with source, blending into one. Thank this constant focus upon you.

6

Feel and give thanks for the abundance of well-being all around. For a full minute.

What 4 things would I like to turn over to the Universe to take care of for me today?

⬅ ➡

1._____
2._____
3._____
4._____

When you stop looking for the desired manifestation, you learn that the feeling grows and carries you to the destination.

Write what things you intend to do today and how you intend to feel as you accomplish these things.

1._____Feeling_____
2._____Feeling_____
3._____Feeling_____
4._____Feeling_____

I look forward to enjoying a productive and fun day.

Pick one of these emotions you would like to use
as today's intended feeling.
Ease, Relaxed, Comfort
Write this feeling here:_____
Now say to yourself...

1.
MY INTENTION IS TO REMIND MYSELF MANY TIMES TODAY...

FOCUSING ON THIS FEELING OF_____ IS MY REAL JOB FOR THE DAY.

2.
MY CURRENT CONDITIONS ARE IRRELEVANT BECAUSE...

I'M CREATING AN ENVIRONMENT THAT IS CAUSING THEM TO CHANGE.

3.
NO MORE SNAPSHOTS OF WHAT IS OR FEELING HELPLESS.

TODAY, I AM GOING TO USE THIS EMOTION AS MY BASE FEELING THAT WILL EFFECT FUTURE OUTCOMES.

Close your eyes again and reach for this intended feeing in place of the feeling of current reality. Notice the softening of your body as you aligning with source.

Write your chosen daily focused emotion reaching for the feeling.

_____ _____ _____
_____ _____ _____
_____ _____ _____
_____ _____ _____

ASK YOURSELF MANY TIMES TODAY
"Is this the attracting vibration, I want the universe to respond to?"
If not, for the count of 10 long breaths in and
slowly letting them out.
Say and feel your chosen emotion in appreciation for the feeling.
It self-creates without any evidence needed.

Write 3 things you would be interested in seeing that just for fun but you are not worried about when.

_____
_____
_____

Let the universe show you these things in playful and exciting ways.

A THOUGHT REACHES A COMBUSTION POINT AT 16 SECONDS.

VIBRATIONAL CASH

A FULL 68 SECONDS ARE EQUIVALENT TO 2 MILLION MAN-HOURS.

Spend Your Vibrational Cash on one thing a day. If wanting a big ticket item slowly pay it off. This will make it more real for you.

The longer you spend feeling like the recipient of this desire the closer you are in being a match to it.

Focus on how it feels to buy this desire and the satisfaction attached within having it. Write about that satisfaction.

Close your eyes again and reach for the first thing that pops into your mind. No matter what the price tag is, big and small creations are all the same. Learn to start treating them all equal.

VIBRATIONALCASH

PAY TO THE ORDER OF

DATE _____

5,000.00

IN YOUR CURRENCY

LIVE THE EXPERIENCE IN THE NOW

FOR _____

SIGN NAME HERE

_____
_____
_____
_____
_____
_____
_____
_____
_____

ASK, BELIEVE,
RECEIVE

ASK

What are ready to take the vibrational journey to?
By asking for this desire it means you are creating a gap and your job is to close it.

BELIEVE/SOURCE

THE MINUTE YOU ASK, IT IS DONE VIBRATIONALLY COMPLETE AND 99.99% DONE PHYSICALLY

RECEIVE:

Create a momentum in belief by feeling it is yours for 20 second, snap shots at a time. Focusing only on feeling not image.

If you hold an emotion as the desire. You no longer are creating an impossibility. The shift from in the future having the desire becomes felt in the present moment, and you will notice the tension has left the solar plexus as you do this.

At this moment you are able to isolate the components of the desire even without having the desire. You become expectant, Being expectant is a very high frequency, and it is one step away from the manifestation to occur.

What do you feel ready to change in your life.
By asking you are now saying "I will deliberately start creating this climate to close the gap.
I am aware of my part in how long the manifestation will take.

_____
_____
_____
_____
_____

Source has now become this vibrationally.
Your work is to create a mimicking or matching vibration.

Faith is created by reaching for the feeling and trusting the manifestation will follow.
Start now creating the feeling it is done by using small 20-second Virtual Realities while conjuring the emotions.
The idea is to preserve the focus that feels good longer, so you can match the frequency and enjoy the pleasures it provides in feelings.
Always leave the imagination
play through, if you feel anything but enjoyment.

POSITIVE ASPECTS

Appreciation is one of the highest vibrations you can use to shift how you are feeling. It will build momentum fast and create an overall positive experience. Even when you are in the worst of moods, if you focus on the parts that you are appreciative for you will begin to start a new point of attraction.

I APPRECIATE YOU!
PERSON
NAME: *WHY?*

_____
_____
_____
_____
_____

I APPRECIATE THE BEAUTY FOUND HERE.
PLACE: *WHY?*

_____
_____
_____
_____
_____

I APPRECIATE THE BEAUTY FOUND HERE.
PLACE: *WHY?*

_____
_____
_____
_____
_____

I APPRECIATE YOU!
PERSON
NAME: *WHY?*

_____
_____
_____
_____
_____

I APPRECIATE HAVING ACCESS TO THIS.
THING: *WHY?*

_____
_____
_____
_____
_____

WHAT I LOVE ABOUT THE WEATHER: *WHY?*

_____
_____
_____
_____
_____

I APPRECIATE YOU!
PERSON
NAME: *WHY?*

_____
_____
_____
_____
_____

I APPRECIATE HAVING ACCESS TO THIS.
THING: *WHY?*

_____
_____
_____
_____
_____

WHAT I LOVE ABOUT..   *WHY?*

_____
_____
_____
_____
_____

POSITIVE
ASPECTS

Focus on anything and everything. Saying "thank you"
Creates more things to be thankful for.

I AM THANKFUL FOR: *WHY?*

_____
_____
_____
_____
_____

I AM THANKFUL FOR: *WHY?*

_____
_____
_____
_____
_____

I AM THANKFUL FOR: *WHY?*

_____
_____
_____
_____
_____

I AM THANKFUL FOR: *WHY?*

_____
_____
_____
_____
_____

I AM THANKFUL FOR: *WHY?*

_____
_____
_____
_____
_____

I AM THANKFUL FOR: *WHY?*

_____
_____
_____
_____
_____

I AM THANKFUL FOR: *WHY?*

_____
_____
_____
_____
_____

I AM THANKFUL FOR: *WHY?*

_____
_____
_____
_____
_____

I AM THANKFUL FOR: *WHY?*

_____
_____
_____
_____
_____

FOODS
yum! WHAT MY BODY ENJOYED TODAY

_____
_____
_____
_____
_____

WATER INTAKE
AM I HYDRATED?

GET PHYSICAL
WHAT MOVEMENT DID MY BODY ENJOY TODAY

_____
_____
_____
_____

MEDITATION
SPEND 15 MINS FOCUSING ON REPETITIVE SOUND. THE MORE BORING IT IS THE BETTER.

A TO Z
WRITE WORDS FROM A TO Z FEELING FOR THEM AS YOU WRITE THEM MAKE UP WORDS IF YOU CANT THINK OF ONE.

A_____ B_____ C_____ D_____

E_____ F_____ G_____ H_____

I_____ J_____ K_____ L_____

M_____ N_____ O_____ P_____

Q_____ R_____ S_____ T_____

U_____ V_____ W_____ X_____

Y_____ Z_____

Am I match _____
If I am feeling ease and comfort in this moment then I am.
I will sit in the feeling of satisfaction at focusing on these emotions right now.

1 SIT FOR ONE MINUTE BREATHING

Focus on holding a smile while taking in long and deep breaths in and slowly letting them out. Relax your body and feel the comfort of where you sit.

2 REMIND YOURSELF HOW IMPORTANT IT IS TO FEEL GOOD.

Today, nothing is more important then I feel good.

3
Write that here:

_____

_____

_____

_____

_____

_____

_____

5 NOTICE HOW THE SUN CAME UP AND THINGS ARE ALWAYS IN MOTION.

4
Close your eyes and see yourself aligning with source, blending into one.
Thank this constant focus upon you.

6
Feel and give thanks for the abundance of well-being all around.
For a full minute.

What 4 things would I like to turn over to the Universe to take care of for me today?

1._____

2._____

3._____

4._____

When you stop looking for the desired manifestation, you learn that the feeling grows and carries you to the destination.

Write what things you intend to do today and how you intend to feel as you accomplish these things.

1._____Feeling_____

2._____Feeling_____

3._____Feeling_____

4._____Feeling_____

I look forward to enjoying a productive and fun day.

Pick one of these emotions you would like to use
as today's intended feeling.
Ease, Relaxed, Comfort
Write this feeling here:_____
Now say to yourself...

**1.
MY INTENTION IS TO
REMIND MYSELF
MANY TIMES
TODAY...**

FOCUSING ON THIS
FEELING OF_____
IS MY REAL
JOB FOR THE DAY.

**2.
MY CURRENT
CONDITIONS ARE
IRRELEVANT
BECAUSE...**

I'M CREATING AN
ENVIRONMENT THAT
IS CAUSING THEM TO
CHANGE.

**3.
NO MORE SNAPSHOTS
OF WHAT IS
OR FEELING HELPLESS.**

TODAY, I AM GOING
TO USE THIS EMOTION
AS MY BASE FEELING
THAT WILL EFFECT
FUTURE OUTCOMES.

Close your eyes again and reach for this intended feeing in
place of the feeling of current reality. Notice the softening
of your body as you aligning with source.

◀━━━━━━━━━━━━━━━━━━━━━━━━━━━▶

Write your chosen daily focused emotion reaching
for the feeling.

_____ _____ _____
_____ _____ _____
_____ _____ _____
_____ _____ _____

ASK YOURSELF MANY TIMES TODAY
"Is this the attracting vibration, I want the universe to respond to?"
If not, for the count of 10 long breaths in and
slowly letting them out.
Say and feel your chosen emotion in appreciation for the feeling.
It self-creates without any evidence needed.

• • • • • • • • • • • • • • •

Write 3 things you would be interested in seeing that just for fun but
you are not worried about when.

_____

_____

_____

Let the universe show you these things in playful and exciting ways.

A THOUGHT REACHES A COMBUSTION POINT AT 16 SECONDS.

Spend Your Vibrational Cash on one thing a day. If wanting a big ticket item slowly pay it off. This will make it more real for you.

VIBRATIONAL CASH

The longer you spend feeling like the recipient of this desire the closer you are in being a match to it.

A FULL 68 SECONDS ARE EQUIVALENT TO 2 MILLION MAN-HOURS.

Focus on how it feels to buy this desire and the satisfaction attached within having it. Write about that satisfaction.

Close your eyes again and reach for the first thing that pops into your mind. No matter what the price tag is, big and small creations are all the same. Learn to start treating them all equal.

VIBRATIONALCASH

DATE _____

PAY TO THE ORDER OF _____

5,000.00

IN YOUR CURRENCY

LIVE THE EXPERIENCE IN THE NOW

FOR _____

SIGN NAME HERE

_____
_____
_____
_____
_____
_____
_____
_____
_____

ASK, BELIEVE,
RECEIVE

ASK

What are ready to take the vibrational journey to?
By asking for this desire it means you are creating a gap and your job is to close it.

BELIEVE/SOURCE

THE MINUTE YOU ASK, IT IS DONE VIBRATIONALLY COMPLETE AND 99.99% DONE PHYSICALLY

RECEIVE:

Create a momentum in belief by feeling it is yours for 20 second, snap shots at a time. Focusing only on feeling not image.

If you hold an emotion as the desire. You no longer are creating an impossibility. The shift from in the future having the desire becomes felt in the present moment, and you will notice the tension has left the solar plexus as you do this.
At this moment you are able to isolate the components of the desire even without having the desire. You become expectant, Being expectant is a very high frequency, and it is one step away from the manifestation to occur.

What do you feel ready to change in your life.
By asking you are now saying "I will deliberately start creating this climate to close the gap.
I am aware of my part in how long the manifestation will take.

_____
_____
_____
_____
_____

Source has now become this vibrationally.
Your work is to create a mimicking or matching vibration.

Faith is created by reaching for the feeling and trusting the manifestation will follow.
Start now creating the feeling it is done by using small 20-second Virtual Realities while conjuring the emotions.
The idea is to preserve the focus that feels good longer, so you can match the frequency and enjoy the pleasures it provides in feelings.
Always leave the imagination play through, if you feel anything but enjoyment.

POSITIVE ASPECTS

Appreciation is one of the highest vibrations you can use to shift how you are feeling.
It will build momentum fast and create an overall positive experience.
Even when you are in the worst of moods, if you focus on the parts that
you are appreciative for you will begin to start a new point of attraction.

I APPRECIATE YOU!
PERSON NAME: *WHY?*

_____
_____
_____
_____
_____

I APPRECIATE THE BEAUTY FOUND HERE.
PLACE: *WHY?*

_____
_____
_____
_____
_____

I APPRECIATE THE BEAUTY FOUND HERE.
PLACE: *WHY?*

_____
_____
_____
_____
_____

I APPRECIATE YOU!
PERSON NAME: *WHY?*

_____
_____
_____
_____

I APPRECIATE HAVING ACCESS TO THIS.
THING: *WHY?*

_____
_____
_____
_____

WHAT I LOVE ABOUT THE WEATHER: *WHY?*

_____
_____
_____
_____

I APPRECIATE YOU!
PERSON NAME: *WHY?*

_____
_____
_____
_____

I APPRECIATE HAVING ACCESS TO THIS.
THING: *WHY?*

_____
_____
_____
_____

WHAT I LOVE ABOUT.. *WHY?*

_____
_____
_____
_____

POSITIVE
ASPECTS

Focus on anything and everything. Saying "thank you"
Creates more things to be thankful for.

I AM THANKFUL FOR:	*WHY?*

I AM THANKFUL FOR:	*WHY?*

I AM THANKFUL FOR:	*WHY?*

I AM THANKFUL FOR:	*WHY?*

I AM THANKFUL FOR:	*WHY?*

I AM THANKFUL FOR:	*WHY?*

I AM THANKFUL FOR:	*WHY?*

I AM THANKFUL FOR:	*WHY?*

I AM THANKFUL FOR:	*WHY?*

FOODS
yum! WHAT MY BODY ENJOYED TODAY

_____
_____
_____
_____
_____
_____

WATER INTAKE
AM I HYDRATED?

GET PHYSICAL
WHAT MOVEMENT DID MY BODY ENJOY TODAY

_____
_____
_____
_____

MEDITATION
SPEND 15 MINS FOCUSING ON REPETITIVE SOUND. THE MORE BORING IT IS THE BETTER.

A TO Z
WRITE WORDS FROM A TO Z FEELING FOR THEM AS YOU WRITE THEM MAKE UP WORDS IF YOU CANT THINK OF ONE.

A_____ B_____ C_____ D_____

E_____ F_____ G_____ H_____

I_____ J_____ K_____ L_____

M_____ N_____ O_____ P_____

Q_____ R_____ S_____ T_____

U_____ V_____ W_____ X_____

Y_____ Z_____

Am I match _____
If I am feeling ease and comfort in this moment then I am.
I will sit in the feeling of satisfaction at focusing on these emotions right now.

1 SIT FOR ONE MINUTE BREATHING

Focus on holding a smile while taking in long and deep breaths in and slowly letting them out. Relax your body and feel the comfort of where you sit.

2 REMIND YOURSELF HOW IMPORTANT IT IS TO FEEL GOOD.

Today, nothing is more important then I feel good.

3

Write that here:

_____
_____
_____
_____
_____
_____
_____

5

NOTICE HOW THE SUN CAME UP AND THINGS ARE ALWAYS IN MOTION.

4

Close your eyes and see yourself aligning with source, blending into one.
Thank this constant focus upon you.

6

Feel and give thanks for the abundance of well-being all around.
For a full minute.

What 4 things would I like to turn over to the Universe to take care of for me today?

1._____
2._____
3._____
4._____

When you stop looking for the desired manifestation, you learn that the feeling grows and carries you to the destination.

Write what things you intend to do today and how you intend to feel as you accomplish these things.

1._____Feeling_____
2._____Feeling_____
3._____Feeling_____
4._____Feeling_____

I look forward to enjoying a productive and fun day.

Pick one of these emotions you would like to use
as today's intended feeling.
Ease, Relaxed, Comfort
Write this feeling here:_____
Now say to yourself...

1.
MY INTENTION IS TO REMIND MYSELF MANY TIMES TODAY...

FOCUSING ON THIS FEELING OF_____ IS MY REAL JOB FOR THE DAY.

2.
MY CURRENT CONDITIONS ARE IRRELEVANT BECAUSE...

I'M CREATING AN ENVIRONMENT THAT IS CAUSING THEM TO CHANGE.

3.
NO MORE SNAPSHOTS OF WHAT IS OR FEELING HELPLESS.

TODAY, I AM GOING TO USE THIS EMOTION AS MY BASE FEELING THAT WILL EFFECT FUTURE OUTCOMES.

Close your eyes again and reach for this intended feeing in place of the feeling of current reality. Notice the softening of your body as you aligning with source.

Write your chosen daily focused emotion reaching
for the feeling.

_____ _____ _____
_____ _____ _____
_____ _____ _____
_____ _____ _____

ASK YOURSELF MANY TIMES TODAY
"Is this the attracting vibration, I want the universe to respond to?"
If not, for the count of 10 long breaths in and
slowly letting them out.
Say and feel your chosen emotion in appreciation for the feeling.
It self-creates without any evidence needed.

Write 3 things you would be interested in seeing that just for fun but
you are not worried about when.

_____
_____
_____

Let the universe show you these things in playful and exciting ways.

A THOUGHT REACHES A COMBUSTION POINT AT 16 SECONDS.

VIBRATIONAL CASH

A FULL 68 SECONDS ARE EQUIVALENT TO 2 MILLION MAN-HOURS.

Spend Your Vibrational Cash on one thing a day. If wanting a big ticket item slowly pay it off. This will make it more real for you.

The longer you spend feeling like the recipient of this desire the closer you are in being a match to it.

Focus on how it feels to buy this desire and the satisfaction attached within having it. Write about that satisfaction.

Close your eyes again and reach for the first thing that pops into your mind. No matter what the price tag is, big and small creations are all the same. Learn to start treating them all equal.

VIBRATIONALCASH

DATE _____

PAY TO THE ORDER OF _____

5,000.00

IN YOUR CURRENCY

LIVE THE EXPERIENCE IN THE NOW

FOR _____

SIGN NAME HERE

_____
_____
_____
_____
_____
_____
_____
_____
_____

ASK, BELIEVE, RECEIVE

ASK

What are ready to take the vibrational journey to?
By asking for this desire it means you are creating a gap and your job is to close it.

BELIEVE/SOURCE

THE MINUTE YOU ASK, IT IS DONE VIBRATIONALLY COMPLETE AND 99.99% DONE PHYSICALLY

RECEIVE:

Create a momentum in belief by feeling it is yours for 20 second, snap shots at a time. Focusing only on feeling not image.

If you hold an emotion as the desire. You no longer are creating an impossibility. The shift from in the future having the desire becomes felt in the present moment, and you will notice the tension has left the solar plexus as you do this.
At this moment you are able to isolate the components of the desire even without having the desire. You become expectant, Being expectant is a very high frequency, and it is one step away from the manifestation to occur.

What do you feel ready to change in your life.
By asking you are now saying "I will deliberately start creating this climate to close the gap.
I am aware of my part in how long the manifestation will take.

_____

_____

_____

_____

_____

Source has now become this vibrationally.
Your work is to create a mimicking or matching vibration.

Faith is created by reaching for the feeling and trusting the manifestation will follow.
Start now creating the feeling it is done by using small 20-second Virtual Realities while conjuring the emotions.
The idea is to preserve the focus that feels good longer, so you can match the frequency and enjoy the pleasures it provides in feelings.
Always leave the imagination play through, if you feel anything but enjoyment.

POSITIVE ASPECTS

Appreciation is one of the highest vibrations you can use to shift how you are feeling.
It will build momentum fast and create an overall positive experience.
Even when you are in the worst of moods, if you focus on the parts that
you are appreciative for you will begin to start a new point of attraction.

I APPRECIATE YOU!
PERSON
NAME: *WHY?*

_____
_____
_____
_____
_____

I APPRECIATE THE BEAUTY FOUND HERE.
PLACE: *WHY?*

_____
_____
_____
_____

I APPRECIATE THE BEAUTY FOUND HERE.
PLACE: *WHY?*

_____
_____
_____
_____

I APPRECIATE YOU!
PERSON
NAME: *WHY?*

_____
_____
_____
_____

I APPRECIATE HAVING ACCESS TO THIS.
THING: *WHY?*

_____
_____
_____
_____

WHAT I LOVE ABOUT THE WEATHER: *WHY?*

_____
_____
_____
_____

I APPRECIATE YOU!
PERSON
NAME: *WHY?*

_____
_____
_____
_____

I APPRECIATE HAVING ACCESS TO THIS.
THING: *WHY?*

_____
_____
_____
_____

WHAT I LOVE ABOUT.. *WHY?*

_____
_____
_____
_____

POSITIVE
ASPECTS

Focus on anything and everything. Saying "thank you"
Creates more things to be thankful for.

I AM THANKFUL
FOR: *WHY?*

_____
_____
_____
_____
_____

I AM THANKFUL
FOR: *WHY?*

_____
_____
_____
_____
_____

I AM THANKFUL
FOR: *WHY?*

_____
_____
_____
_____
_____

I AM THANKFUL
FOR: *WHY?*

_____
_____
_____
_____
_____

I AM THANKFUL
FOR: *WHY?*

_____
_____
_____
_____
_____

I AM THANKFUL *WHY?*
FOR:

_____
_____
_____
_____
_____

I AM THANKFUL
FOR: *WHY?*

_____
_____
_____
_____

I AM THANKFUL
FOR: *WHY?*

_____
_____
_____
_____

I AM THANKFUL
FOR: *WHY?*

_____
_____
_____
_____

FOODS
yum! WHAT MY BODY ENJOYED TODAY

_____
_____
_____
_____
_____
_____

WATER INTAKE
AM I HYDRATED?

GET PHYSICAL
WHAT MOVEMENT DID MY BODY ENJOY TODAY

_____
_____
_____
_____
_____

MEDITATION

SPEND 15 MINS FOCUSING ON REPETITIVE SOUND. THE MORE BORING IT IS THE BETTER.

A TO Z

WRITE WORDS FROM A TO Z FEELING FOR THEM AS YOU WRITE THEM MAKE UP WORDS IF YOU CANT THINK OF ONE.

A_____ B_____ C_____ D_____

E_____ F_____ G_____ H_____

I_____ J_____ K_____ L_____

M_____ N_____ O_____ P_____

Q_____ R_____ S_____ T_____

U_____ V_____ W_____ X_____

Y_____ Z_____

Am I match _____
If I am feeling ease and comfort in this moment then I am.
I will sit in the feeling of satisfaction at focusing on these emotions right now.

1 SIT FOR ONE MINUTE BREATHING

Focus on holding a smile while taking in long and deep breaths in and slowly letting them out. Relax your body and feel the comfort of where you sit.

2 REMIND YOURSELF HOW IMPORTANT IT IS TO FEEL GOOD.

Today, nothing is more important then I feel good.

3

Write that here:

_____

_____

_____

_____

_____

_____

5 NOTICE HOW THE SUN CAME UP AND THINGS ARE ALWAYS IN MOTION.

4

Close your eyes and see yourself aligning with source, blending into one.
Thank this constant focus upon you.

6

Feel and give thanks for the abundance of well-being all around.
For a full minute.

What 4 things would I like to turn over to the Universe to take care of for me today?

1._____

2._____

3._____

4._____

When you stop looking for the desired manifestation, you learn that the feeling grows and carries you to the destination.

Write what things you intend to do today and how you intend to feel as you accomplish these things.

1._____Feeling_____

2._____Feeling_____

3._____Feeling_____

4._____Feeling_____

I look forward to enjoying a productive and fun day.

Pick one of these emotions you would like to use
as today's intended feeling.
Ease, Relaxed, Comfort
Write this feeling here:_____
Now say to yourself...

1.
MY INTENTION IS TO REMIND MYSELF MANY TIMES TODAY...

FOCUSING ON THIS FEELING OF_____ IS MY REAL JOB FOR THE DAY.

2.
MY CURRENT CONDITIONS ARE IRRELEVANT BECAUSE...

I'M CREATING AN ENVIRONMENT THAT IS CAUSING THEM TO CHANGE.

3.
NO MORE SNAPSHOTS OF WHAT IS OR FEELING HELPLESS.

TODAY, I AM GOING TO USE THIS EMOTION AS MY BASE FEELING THAT WILL EFFECT FUTURE OUTCOMES.

Close your eyes again and reach for this intended feeing in place of the feeling of current reality. Notice the softening of your body as you aligning with source.

◀━━━━━━━━━━━━━━━━━━━━━━━━━━━━━━━▶

Write your chosen daily focused emotion reaching
for the feeling.

_____ _____ _____
_____ _____ _____
_____ _____ _____
_____ _____ _____

ASK YOURSELF MANY TIMES TODAY
"Is this the attracting vibration, I want the universe to respond to?"
If not, for the count of 10 long breaths in and
slowly letting them out.
Say and feel your chosen emotion in appreciation for the feeling.
It self-creates without any evidence needed.

Write 3 things you would be interested in seeing that just for fun but
you are not worried about when.

_____
_____
_____

Let the universe show you these things in playful and exciting ways.

A THOUGHT REACHES A COMBUSTION POINT AT 16 SECONDS.

VIBRATIONAL CASH

A FULL 68 SECONDS ARE EQUIVALENT TO 2 MILLION MAN-HOURS.

Spend Your Vibrational Cash on one thing a day. If wanting a big ticket item slowly pay it off. This will make it more real for you.

The longer you spend feeling like the recipient of this desire the closer you are in being a match to it.

Focus on how it feels to buy this desire and the satisfaction attached within having it. Write about that satisfaction.

Close your eyes again and reach for the first thing that pops into your mind. No matter what the price tag is, big and small creations are all the same. Learn to start treating them all equal.

VibrationalCash

Date _____

PAY TO THE ORDER OF _____

5,000.00

IN YOUR CURRENCY

LIVE THE EXPERIENCE IN THE NOW

FOR _____

SIGN NAME HERE _____

_____
_____
_____
_____
_____
_____
_____
_____
_____

ASK, BELIEVE,
RECEIVE

ASK

What are ready to take the vibrational journey to?
By asking for this desire it means you are creating a gap and your job is to close it.

BELIEVE/SOURCE

THE MINUTE YOU ASK, IT IS DONE VIBRATIONALLY COMPLETE AND 99.99% DONE PHYSICALLY

RECEIVE:

Create a momentum in belief by feeling it is yours for 20 second, snap shots at a time. Focusing only on feeling not image.

If you hold an emotion as the desire. You no longer are creating an impossibility. The shift from in the future having the desire becomes felt in the present moment, and you will notice the tension has left the solar plexus as you do this.
At this moment you are able to isolate the components of the desire even without having the desire. You become expectant, Being expectant is a very high frequency, and it is one step away from the manifestation to occur.

What do you feel ready to change in your life.
By asking you are now saying "I will deliberately start creating this climate to close the gap.
I am aware of my part in how long the manifestation will take.

_____

_____

_____

_____

_____

Source has now become this vibrationally.
Your work is to create a mimicking or matching vibration.

Faith is created by reaching for the feeling and trusting the manifestation will follow.
Start now creating the feeling it is done by using small 20-second Virtual Realities while conjuring the emotions.
The idea is to preserve the focus that feels good longer, so you can match the frequency and enjoy the pleasures it provides in feelings.
Always leave the imagination play through, if you feel anything but enjoyment.

POSITIVE ASPECTS

Appreciation is one of the highest vibrations you can use to shift how you are feeling.
It will build momentum fast and create an overall positive experience.
Even when you are in the worst of moods, if you focus on the parts that
you are appreciative for you will begin to start a new point of attraction.

I APPRECIATE YOU!
PERSON
NAME: *WHY?*

_____
_____
_____
_____
_____

I APPRECIATE THE
BEAUTY FOUND HERE.
PLACE: *WHY?*

_____
_____
_____
_____
_____

I APPRECIATE THE
BEAUTY FOUND HERE.
PLACE: *WHY?*

_____
_____
_____
_____
_____

I APPRECIATE YOU!
PERSON
NAME: *WHY?*

_____
_____
_____
_____

I APPRECIATE HAVING
ACCESS TO THIS.   *WHY?*
THING:

_____
_____
_____
_____

WHAT I LOVE ABOUT
THE WEATHER: *WHY?*

_____
_____
_____
_____

I APPRECIATE YOU!
PERSON
NAME: *WHY?*

_____
_____
_____
_____

I APPRECIATE HAVING
ACCESS TO THIS.   *WHY?*
THING:

_____
_____
_____
_____

WHAT I LOVE ABOUT..
              WHY?

_____
_____
_____
_____

POSITIVE
ASPECTS

Focus on anything and everything. Saying "thank you"
Creates more things to be thankful for.

I AM THANKFUL FOR: *WHY?*

_____
_____
_____
_____

I AM THANKFUL FOR: *WHY?*

_____
_____
_____
_____

I AM THANKFUL FOR: *WHY?*

_____
_____
_____
_____

I AM THANKFUL FOR: *WHY?*

_____
_____
_____
_____
_____

I AM THANKFUL FOR: *WHY?*

_____
_____
_____
_____
_____

I AM THANKFUL FOR: *WHY?*

_____
_____
_____
_____
_____

I AM THANKFUL FOR: *WHY?*

_____
_____
_____
_____

I AM THANKFUL FOR: *WHY?*

_____
_____
_____
_____

I AM THANKFUL FOR: *WHY?*

_____
_____
_____
_____

FOODS
yum! WHAT MY BODY ENJOYED TODAY

_____
_____
_____
_____
_____
_____

WATER INTAKE ✓
AM I HYDRATED?

GET PHYSICAL
WHAT MOVEMENT DID MY BODY ENJOY TODAY

_____
_____
_____
_____

MEDITATION

SPEND 15 MINS FOCUSING ON REPETITIVE SOUND. THE MORE BORING IT IS THE BETTER.

A TO Z

WRITE WORDS FROM A TO Z FEELING FOR THEM AS YOU WRITE THEM MAKE UP WORDS IF YOU CANT THINK OF ONE.

A_____ B_____ C_____ D_____

E_____ F_____ G_____ H_____

I_____ J_____ K_____ L_____

M_____ N_____ O_____ P_____

Q_____ R_____ S_____ T_____

U_____ V_____ W_____ X_____

Y_____ Z_____

Am I match ____
If I am feeling ease and comfort in this moment then I am.
I will sit in the feeling of satisfaction at focusing on these emotions right now.

1 SIT FOR ONE MINUTE BREATHING

Focus on holding a smile while taking in long and deep breaths in and slowly letting them out. Relax your body and feel the comfort of where you sit.

2 REMIND YOURSELF HOW IMPORTANT IT IS TO FEEL GOOD.

Today, nothing is more important then I feel good.

3 Write that here:

_____
_____
_____
_____
_____
_____
_____

5 NOTICE HOW THE SUN CAME UP AND THINGS ARE ALWAYS IN MOTION.

4 Close your eyes and see yourself aligning with source, blending into one. Thank this constant focus upon you.

6 Feel and give thanks for the abundance of well-being all around. For a full minute.

What 4 things would I like to turn over to the Universe to take care of for me today?

1._____
2._____
3._____
4._____

When you stop looking for the desired manifestation, you learn that the feeling grows and carries you to the destination.

Write what things you intend to do today and how you intend to feel as you accomplish these things.

1._____Feeling_____
2._____Feeling_____
3._____Feeling_____
4._____Feeling_____

I look forward to enjoying a productive and fun day.

Pick one of these emotions you would like to use
as today's intended feeling.
Ease, Relaxed, Comfort
Write this feeling here:_____
Now say to yourself...

1.
MY INTENTION IS TO REMIND MYSELF MANY TIMES TODAY...

FOCUSING ON THIS FEELING OF_____ IS MY REAL JOB FOR THE DAY.

2.
MY CURRENT CONDITIONS ARE IRRELEVANT BECAUSE...

I'M CREATING AN ENVIRONMENT THAT IS CAUSING THEM TO CHANGE.

3.
NO MORE SNAPSHOTS OF WHAT IS OR FEELING HELPLESS.

TODAY, I AM GOING TO USE THIS EMOTION AS MY BASE FEELING THAT WILL EFFECT FUTURE OUTCOMES.

Close your eyes again and reach for this intended feeing in place of the feeling of current reality. Notice the softening of your body as you aligning with source.

Write your chosen daily focused emotion reaching for the feeling.

_____ _____ _____
_____ _____ _____
_____ _____ _____
_____ _____ _____

ASK YOURSELF MANY TIMES TODAY
"Is this the attracting vibration, I want the universe to respond to?"
If not, for the count of 10 long breaths in and
slowly letting them out.
Say and feel your chosen emotion in appreciation for the feeling.
It self-creates without any evidence needed.

Write 3 things you would be interested in seeing that just for fun but you are not worried about when.

_____
_____
_____

Let the universe show you these things in playful and exciting ways.

A THOUGHT REACHES A COMBUSTION POINT AT 16 SECONDS.

VIBRATIONAL CASH

A FULL 68 SECONDS ARE EQUIVALENT TO 2 MILLION MAN-HOURS.

Spend Your Vibrational Cash on one thing a day. If wanting a big ticket item slowly pay it off. This will make it more real for you.

The longer you spend feeling like the recipient of this desire the closer you are in being a match to it.

Focus on how it feels to buy this desire and the satisfaction attached within having it. Write about that satisfaction.

Close your eyes again and reach for the first thing that pops into your mind. No matter what the price tag is, big and small creations are all the same. Learn to start treating them all equal.

VIBRATIONALCASH

PAY TO
THE ORDER OF

DATE

5,000.00

IN YOUR CURRENCY

LIVE THE EXPERIENCE IN THE NOW

FOR

SIGN NAME HERE

ASK, BELIEVE,
RECEIVE

ASK

What are ready to take the vibrational journey to?
By asking for this desire it means you are creating a gap and your job is to close it.

BELIEVE/SOURCE

THE MINUTE YOU ASK, IT IS DONE VIBRATIONALLY COMPLETE AND 99.99% DONE PHYSICALLY

RECEIVE:

Create a momentum in belief by feeling it is yours for 20 second, snap shots at a time. Focusing only on feeling not image.

If you hold an emotion as the desire. You no longer are creating an impossibility. The shift from in the future having the desire becomes felt in the present moment, and you will notice the tension has left the solar plexus as you do this.
At this moment you are able to isolate the components of the desire even without having the desire. You become expectant, Being expectant is a very high frequency, and it is one step away from the manifestation to occur.

What do you feel ready to change in your life.
By asking you are now saying "I will deliberately start creating this climate to close the gap.
I am aware of my part in how long the manifestation will take.

_____
_____
_____
_____
_____

Source has now become this vibrationally.
Your work is to create a mimicking or matching vibration.

Faith is created by reaching for the feeling and trusting the manifestation will follow.
Start now creating the feeling it is done by using small 20-second Virtual Realities while conjuring the emotions.
The idea is to preserve the focus that feels good longer, so you can match the frequency and enjoy the pleasures it provides in feelings.
Always leave the imagination play through, if you feel anything but enjoyment.

POSITIVE ASPECTS

Appreciation is one of the highest vibrations you can use to shift how you are feeling.
It will build momentum fast and create an overall positive experience.
Even when you are in the worst of moods, if you focus on the parts that
you are appreciative for you will begin to start a new point of attraction.

I APPRECIATE YOU!
PERSON
NAME: *WHY?*

_____
_____
_____
_____
_____

I APPRECIATE THE
BEAUTY FOUND HERE.
PLACE: *WHY?*

_____
_____
_____
_____
_____

I APPRECIATE THE
BEAUTY FOUND HERE.
PLACE: *WHY?*

_____
_____
_____
_____
_____

I APPRECIATE YOU!
PERSON
NAME: *WHY?*

_____
_____
_____
_____
_____

I APPRECIATE HAVING
ACCESS TO THIS.
THING: *WHY?*

_____
_____
_____
_____
_____

WHAT I LOVE ABOUT
THE WEATHER: *WHY?*

_____
_____
_____
_____
_____

I APPRECIATE YOU!
PERSON
NAME: *WHY?*

_____
_____
_____
_____
_____

I APPRECIATE HAVING
ACCESS TO THIS.
THING: *WHY?*

_____
_____
_____
_____
_____

WHAT I LOVE ABOUT..
                       WHY?

_____
_____
_____
_____
_____

POSITIVE
ASPECTS

Focus on anything and everything. Saying "thank you"
Creates more things to be thankful for.

I AM THANKFUL
FOR: *WHY?*

_____
_____
_____
_____
_____

I AM THANKFUL
FOR: *WHY?*

_____
_____
_____
_____
_____

I AM THANKFUL
FOR: *WHY?*

_____
_____
_____
_____
_____

I AM THANKFUL
FOR: *WHY?*

_____
_____
_____
_____
_____

I AM THANKFUL
FOR: *WHY?*

_____
_____
_____
_____
_____

I AM THANKFUL *WHY?*
FOR:

_____
_____
_____
_____
_____

I AM THANKFUL
FOR: *WHY?*

_____
_____
_____
_____
_____

I AM THANKFUL
FOR: *WHY?*

_____
_____
_____
_____
_____

I AM THANKFUL
FOR: *WHY?*

_____
_____
_____
_____
_____

FOODS
yum! WHAT MY BODY ENJOYED TODAY

_____
_____
_____
_____
_____
_____

WATER INTAKE
AM I HYDRATED?

GET PHYSICAL
WHAT MOVEMENT DID MY BODY ENJOY TODAY

_____
_____
_____
_____

MEDITATION

SPEND 15 MINS FOCUSING ON REPETITIVE SOUND. THE MORE BORING IT IS THE BETTER.

A TO Z

WRITE WORDS FROM A TO Z FEELING FOR THEM AS YOU WRITE THEM MAKE UP WORDS IF YOU CANT THINK OF ONE.

A_____ B_____ C_____ D_____

E_____ F_____ G_____ H_____

I_____ J_____ K_____ L_____

M_____ N_____ O_____ P_____

Q_____ R_____ S_____ T_____

U_____ V_____ W_____ X_____

Y_____ Z_____

Am I match ____
If I am feeling ease and comfort in this moment then I am.
I will sit in the feeling of satisfaction at focusing on these emotions right now.

1 SIT FOR ONE MINUTE BREATHING

Focus on holding a smile while taking in long and deep breaths in and slowly letting them out. Relax your body and feel the comfort of where you sit.

2 REMIND YOURSELF HOW IMPORTANT IT IS TO FEEL GOOD.

Today, nothing is more important then I feel good.

3

Write that here:

_____

_____

_____

_____

_____

_____

_____

4

Close your eyes and see yourself aligning with source, blending into one.
Thank this constant focus upon you.

5

NOTICE HOW THE SUN CAME UP AND THINGS ARE ALWAYS IN MOTION.

6

Feel and give thanks for the abundance of well-being all around.
For a full minute.

What 4 things would I like to turn over to the Universe to take care of for me today?

1._____

2._____

3._____

4._____

When you stop looking for the desired manifestation, you learn that the feeling grows and carries you to the destination.

Write what things you intend to do today
and how you intend to feel as you accomplish these things.

1._____Feeling_____

2._____Feeling_____

3._____Feeling_____

4._____Feeling_____

I look forward to enjoying a productive and fun day.

Pick one of these emotions you would like to use
as today's intended feeling.
Ease, Relaxed, Comfort
Write this feeling here:_____
Now say to yourself...

1.
MY INTENTION IS TO REMIND MYSELF MANY TIMES TODAY...

FOCUSING ON THIS FEELING OF_____ IS MY REAL JOB FOR THE DAY.

2.
MY CURRENT CONDITIONS ARE IRRELEVANT BECAUSE...

I'M CREATING AN ENVIRONMENT THAT IS CAUSING THEM TO CHANGE.

3.
NO MORE SNAPSHOTS OF WHAT IS OR FEELING HELPLESS.

TODAY, I AM GOING TO USE THIS EMOTION AS MY BASE FEELING THAT WILL EFFECT FUTURE OUTCOMES.

Close your eyes again and reach for this intended feeing in place of the feeling of current reality. Notice the softening of your body as you aligning with source.

Write your chosen daily focused emotion reaching for the feeling.

_____ _____ _____
_____ _____ _____
_____ _____ _____
_____ _____ _____

ASK YOURSELF MANY TIMES TODAY
"Is this the attracting vibration, I want the universe to respond to?"
If not, for the count of 10 long breaths in and
slowly letting them out.
Say and feel your chosen emotion in appreciation for the feeling.
It self-creates without any evidence needed.

Write 3 things you would be interested in seeing that just for fun but you are not worried about when.

_____
_____
_____

Let the universe show you these things in playful and exciting ways.

A THOUGHT REACHES A COMBUSTION POINT AT 16 SECONDS.

Spend Your Vibrational Cash on one thing a day. If wanting a big ticket item slowly pay it off. This will make it more real for you.

VIBRATIONAL
CASH

The longer you spend feeling like the recipient of this desire the closer you are in being a match to it.

A FULL 68 SECONDS ARE EQUIVALENT TO 2 MILLION MAN-HOURS.

Focus on how it feels to buy this desire and the satisfaction attached within having it. Write about that satisfaction.

Close your eyes again and reach for the first thing that pops into your mind. No matter what the price tag is, big and small creations are all the same. Learn to start treating them all equal.

VIBRATIONALCASH

DATE _____

PAY TO
THE ORDER OF

5,000.00

IN YOUR CURRENCY

_____

LIVE THE EXPERIENCE IN THE NOW

FOR _____

SIGN NAME HERE

_____

_____

_____

_____

_____

_____

_____

_____

_____

ASK, BELIEVE,
RECEIVE

ASK

What are ready to take the vibrational journey to?
By asking for this desire it means you are creating a gap and your job is to close it.

BELIEVE/SOURCE

THE MINUTE YOU ASK, IT IS DONE VIBRATIONALLY COMPLETE AND 99.99% DONE PHYSICALLY

RECEIVE:

Create a momentum in belief by feeling it is yours for 20 second, snap shots at a time. Focusing only on feeling not image.

If you hold an emotion as the desire. You no longer are creating an impossibility. The shift from in the future having the desire becomes felt in the present moment, and you will notice the tension has left the solar plexus as you do this.
At this moment you are able to isolate the components of the desire even without having the desire. You become expectant, Being expectant is a very high frequency, and it is one step away from the manifestation to occur.

What do you feel ready to change in your life.
By asking you are now saying "I will deliberately start creating this climate to close the gap.
I am aware of my part in how long the manifestation will take.

_____
_____
_____
_____
_____

Source has now become this vibrationally.
Your work is to create a mimicking or matching vibration.

Faith is created by reaching for the feeling and trusting the manifestation will follow.
Start now creating the feeling it is done by using small 20-second Virtual Realities while conjuring the emotions.
The idea is to preserve the focus that feels good longer, so you can match the frequency and enjoy the pleasures it provides in feelings.
Always leave the imagination
play through, if you feel anything but enjoyment.

POSITIVE ASPECTS

Appreciation is one of the highest vibrations you can use to shift how you are feeling.
It will build momentum fast and create an overall positive experience.
Even when you are in the worst of moods, if you focus on the parts that
you are appreciative for you will begin to start a new point of attraction.

I APPRECIATE YOU!
PERSON
NAME: *WHY?*

_____
_____
_____
_____
_____

I APPRECIATE THE BEAUTY FOUND HERE.
PLACE: *WHY?*

_____
_____
_____
_____
_____

I APPRECIATE THE BEAUTY FOUND HERE.
PLACE: *WHY?*

_____
_____
_____
_____
_____

I APPRECIATE YOU!
PERSON
NAME: *WHY?*

_____
_____
_____
_____
_____

I APPRECIATE HAVING ACCESS TO THIS.
THING: *WHY?*

_____
_____
_____
_____
_____

WHAT I LOVE ABOUT THE WEATHER: *WHY?*

_____
_____
_____
_____
_____

I APPRECIATE YOU!
PERSON
NAME: *WHY?*

_____
_____
_____
_____

I APPRECIATE HAVING ACCESS TO THIS.
THING: *WHY?*

_____
_____
_____
_____

WHAT I LOVE ABOUT.. *WHY?*

_____
_____
_____
_____

POSITIVE ASPECTS

Focus on anything and everything. Saying "thank you"
Creates more things to be thankful for.

I AM THANKFUL
FOR: *WHY?*

_____
_____
_____
_____
_____

I AM THANKFUL
FOR: *WHY?*

_____
_____
_____
_____
_____

I AM THANKFUL
FOR: *WHY?*

_____
_____
_____
_____
_____

I AM THANKFUL
FOR: *WHY?*

_____
_____
_____
_____
_____

I AM THANKFUL
FOR: *WHY?*

_____
_____
_____
_____
_____

I AM THANKFUL *WHY?*
FOR:

_____
_____
_____
_____
_____

I AM THANKFUL
FOR: *WHY?*

_____
_____
_____
_____

I AM THANKFUL
FOR: *WHY?*

_____
_____
_____
_____

I AM THANKFUL
FOR: *WHY?*

_____
_____
_____
_____

FOODS
yum! WHAT MY BODY
ENJOYED TODAY

_____
_____
_____
_____
_____
_____

WATER INTAKE

AM I
HYDRATED?

GET PHYSICAL

WHAT
MOVEMENT DID MY
BODY ENJOY TODAY

_____
_____
_____
_____

MEDITATION

SPEND 15 MINS FOCUSING
ON REPETITIVE SOUND.
THE MORE BORING IT IS THE
BETTER.

A TO Z

WRITE WORDS FROM A TO Z
FEELING FOR THEM AS YOU
WRITE THEM MAKE UP
WORDS IF YOU CANT THINK
OF ONE.

A_____ B_____ C_____ D_____

E_____ F_____ G_____ H_____

I_____ J_____ K_____ L_____

M_____ N_____ O_____ P_____

Q_____ R_____ S_____ T_____

U_____ V_____ W_____ X_____

Y_____ Z_____

Am I match ____
If I am feeling ease and comfort in this moment then I am.
I will sit in the feeling of satisfaction at focusing on these emotions right
now.

1 SIT FOR ONE MINUTE BREATHING

Focus on holding a smile while taking in long and deep breaths in and slowly letting them out. Relax your body and feel the comfort of where you sit.

2 REMIND YOURSELF HOW IMPORTANT IT IS TO FEEL GOOD.

Today, nothing is more important then I feel good.

3

Write that here:

_____
_____
_____
_____
_____
_____

5 NOTICE HOW THE SUN CAME UP AND THINGS ARE ALWAYS IN MOTION.

4

Close your eyes and see yourself aligning with source, blending into one.
Thank this constant focus upon you.

6

Feel and give thanks for the abundance of well-being all around.
For a full minute.

What 4 things would I like to turn over to the Universe to take care of for me today?

1._____
2._____
3._____
4._____

When you stop looking for the desired manifestation, you learn that the feeling grows and carries you to the destination.

Write what things you intend to do today and how you intend to feel as you accomplish these things.

1._____Feeling_____
2._____Feeling_____
3._____Feeling_____
4._____Feeling_____

I look forward to enjoying a productive and fun day.

Pick one of these emotions you would like to use
as today's intended feeling.
Ease, Relaxed, Comfort
Write this feeling here:_____
Now say to yourself...

1.
MY INTENTION IS TO REMIND MYSELF MANY TIMES TODAY...

FOCUSING ON THIS FEELING OF_____ IS MY REAL JOB FOR THE DAY.

2.
MY CURRENT CONDITIONS ARE IRRELEVANT BECAUSE...

I'M CREATING AN ENVIRONMENT THAT IS CAUSING THEM TO CHANGE.

3.
NO MORE SNAPSHOTS OF WHAT IS OR FEELING HELPLESS.

TODAY, I AM GOING TO USE THIS EMOTION AS MY BASE FEELING THAT WILL EFFECT FUTURE OUTCOMES.

Close your eyes again and reach for this intended feeing in place of the feeling of current reality. Notice the softening of your body as you aligning with source.

Write your chosen daily focused emotion reaching for the feeling.

_____ _____ _____
_____ _____ _____
_____ _____ _____
_____ _____ _____

ASK YOURSELF MANY TIMES TODAY
"Is this the attracting vibration, I want the universe to respond to?"
If not, for the count of 10 long breaths in and
slowly letting them out.
Say and feel your chosen emotion in appreciation for the feeling.
It self-creates without any evidence needed.

Write 3 things you would be interested in seeing that just for fun but you are not worried about when.

_____
_____
_____

Let the universe show you these things in playful and exciting ways.

A THOUGHT REACHES A COMBUSTION POINT AT 16 SECONDS.

Spend Your Vibrational Cash on one thing a day. If wanting a big ticket item slowly pay it off. This will make it more real for you.

VIBRATIONAL CASH

The longer you spend feeling like the recipient of this desire the closer you are in being a match to it.

A FULL 68 SECONDS ARE EQUIVALENT TO 2 MILLION MAN-HOURS.

Focus on how it feels to buy this desire and the satisfaction attached within having it. Write about that satisfaction.

Close your eyes again and reach for the first thing that pops into your mind. No matter what the price tag is, big and small creations are all the same. Learn to start treating them all equal.

VIBRATIONALCASH

DATE _____

PAY TO
THE ORDER OF

5,000.00

IN YOUR CURRENCY

_____

LIVE THE EXPERIENCE IN THE NOW

FOR _____

SIGN NAME HERE

_____
_____
_____
_____
_____
_____
_____
_____
_____
_____

ASK, BELIEVE,
RECEIVE

ASK

What are ready to take the vibrational journey to?
By asking for this desire it means you are creating a gap and your job is to close it.

BELIEVE/SOURCE

THE MINUTE YOU ASK, IT IS DONE VIBRATIONALLY COMPLETE AND 99.99% DONE PHYSICALLY

RECEIVE:

Create a momentum in belief by feeling it is yours for 20 second, snap shots at a time. Focusing only on feeling not image.

If you hold an emotion as the desire. You no longer are creating an impossibility. The shift from in the future having the desire becomes felt in the present moment, and you will notice the tension has left the solar plexus as you do this. At this moment you are able to isolate the components of the desire even without having the desire. You become expectant, Being expectant is a very high frequency, and it is one step away from the manifestation to occur.

What do you feel ready to change in your life.
By asking you are now saying "I will deliberately start creating this climate to close the gap. I am aware of my part in how long the manifestation will take.

_____
_____
_____
_____
_____

Source has now become this vibrationally.
Your work is to create a mimicking or matching vibration.

Faith is created by reaching for the feeling and trusting the manifestation will follow.
Start now creating the feeling it is done by using small 20-second Virtual Realities while conjuring the emotions.
The idea is to preserve the focus that feels good longer, so you can match the frequency and enjoy the pleasures it provides in feelings.
Always leave the imagination play through, if you feel anything but enjoyment.

POSITIVE ASPECTS

Appreciation is one of the highest vibrations you can use to shift how you are feeling.
It will build momentum fast and create an overall positive experience.
Even when you are in the worst of moods, if you focus on the parts that
you are appreciative for you will begin to start a new point of attraction.

I APPRECIATE YOU!
PERSON
NAME: *WHY?*

_____
_____
_____
_____
_____

I APPRECIATE THE
BEAUTY FOUND HERE.
PLACE: *WHY?*

_____
_____
_____
_____
_____

I APPRECIATE THE
BEAUTY FOUND HERE.
PLACE: *WHY?*

_____
_____
_____
_____
_____

I APPRECIATE YOU!
PERSON
NAME: *WHY?*

_____
_____
_____
_____

I APPRECIATE HAVING
ACCESS TO THIS.
THING: *WHY?*

_____
_____
_____
_____

WHAT I LOVE ABOUT
THE WEATHER: *WHY?*

_____
_____
_____
_____

I APPRECIATE YOU!
PERSON
NAME: *WHY?*

_____
_____
_____
_____

I APPRECIATE HAVING
ACCESS TO THIS.
THING: *WHY?*

_____
_____
_____
_____

WHAT I LOVE ABOUT..
                          WHY?

_____
_____
_____
_____

POSITIVE
ASPECTS

Focus on anything and everything. Saying "thank you"
Creates more things to be thankful for.

I AM THANKFUL FOR: *WHY?*

_____
_____
_____
_____
_____

I AM THANKFUL FOR: *WHY?*

_____
_____
_____
_____
_____

I AM THANKFUL FOR: *WHY?*

_____
_____
_____
_____
_____

I AM THANKFUL FOR: *WHY?*

_____
_____
_____
_____
_____

I AM THANKFUL FOR: *WHY?*

_____
_____
_____
_____
_____

I AM THANKFUL FOR: *WHY?*

_____
_____
_____
_____
_____

I AM THANKFUL FOR: *WHY?*

_____
_____
_____
_____
_____

I AM THANKFUL FOR: *WHY?*

_____
_____
_____
_____
_____

I AM THANKFUL FOR: *WHY?*

_____
_____
_____
_____
_____

FOODS
yum! WHAT MY BODY ENJOYED TODAY

_____
_____
_____
_____
_____
_____
_____

WATER INTAKE
AM I HYDRATED?

GET PHYSICAL
WHAT MOVEMENT DID MY BODY ENJOY TODAY

_____
_____
_____
_____
_____

MEDITATION

SPEND 15 MINS FOCUSING ON REPETITIVE SOUND. THE MORE BORING IT IS THE BETTER.

A TO Z

WRITE WORDS FROM A TO Z FEELING FOR THEM AS YOU WRITE THEM MAKE UP WORDS IF YOU CANT THINK OF ONE.

A_____ B_____ C_____ D_____

E_____ F_____ G_____ H_____

I_____ J_____ K_____ L_____

M_____ N_____ O_____ P_____

Q_____ R_____ S_____ T_____

U_____ V_____ W_____ X_____

Y_____ Z_____

Am I match ____
If I am feeling ease and comfort in this moment then I am.
I will sit in the feeling of satisfaction at focusing on these emotions right now.

1 SIT FOR ONE MINUTE BREATHING

Focus on holding a smile while taking in long and deep breaths in and slowly letting them out. Relax your body and feel the comfort of where you sit.

2 REMIND YOURSELF HOW IMPORTANT IT IS TO FEEL GOOD.

Today, nothing is more important then I feel good.

3
Write that here:

_____

_____

_____

_____

_____

_____

5
NOTICE HOW THE SUN CAME UP AND THINGS ARE ALWAYS IN MOTION.

4
Close your eyes and see yourself aligning with source, blending into one. Thank this constant focus upon you.

6
Feel and give thanks for the abundance of well-being all around. For a full minute.

What 4 things would I like to turn over to the Universe to take care of for me today?

1._____
2._____
3._____
4._____

When you stop looking for the desired manifestation, you learn that the feeling grows and carries you to the destination.

Write what things you intend to do today and how you intend to feel as you accomplish these things.

1._____Feeling_____
2._____Feeling_____
3._____Feeling_____
4._____Feeling_____

I look forward to enjoying a productive and fun day.

Pick one of these emotions you would like to use
as today's intended feeling.
Ease, Relaxed, Comfort
Write this feeling here:_____
Now say to yourself...

**1.
MY INTENTION IS TO
REMIND MYSELF
MANY TIMES
TODAY...**

FOCUSING ON THIS
FEELING OF_____
IS MY REAL
JOB FOR THE DAY.

**2.
MY CURRENT
CONDITIONS ARE
IRRELEVANT
BECAUSE...**

I'M CREATING AN
ENVIRONMENT THAT
IS CAUSING THEM TO
CHANGE.

**3.
NO MORE SNAPSHOTS
OF WHAT IS
OR FEELING HELPLESS.**

TODAY, I AM GOING
TO USE THIS EMOTION
AS MY BASE FEELING
THAT WILL EFFECT
FUTURE OUTCOMES.

Close your eyes again and reach for this intended feeing in
place of the feeling of current reality. Notice the softening
of your body as you aligning with source.

◄───►

Write your chosen daily focused emotion reaching
for the feeling.

_____ _____ _____
_____ _____ _____
_____ _____ _____
_____ _____ _____

ASK YOURSELF MANY TIMES TODAY
"Is this the attracting vibration, I want the universe to respond to?"
If not, for the count of 10 long breaths in and
slowly letting them out.
Say and feel your chosen emotion in appreciation for the feeling.
It self-creates without any evidence needed.

• • • • • • • • • • • • • • • • •

Write 3 things you would be interested in seeing that just for fun but
you are not worried about when.

_____
_____
_____

Let the universe show you these things in playful and exciting ways.

A THOUGHT REACHES A COMBUSTION POINT AT 16 SECONDS.

VIBRATIONAL
CASH

A FULL 68 SECONDS ARE EQUIVALENT TO 2 MILLION MAN-HOURS.

Spend Your Vibrational Cash on one thing a day. If wanting a big ticket item slowly pay it off. This will make it more real for you.

The longer you spend feeling like the recipient of this desire the closer you are in being a match to it.

Focus on how it feels to buy this desire and the satisfaction attached within having it. Write about that satisfaction.

Close your eyes again and reach for the first thing that pops into your mind. No matter what the price tag is, big and small creations are all the same. Learn to start treating them all equal.

VIBRATIONALCASH

DATE

PAY TO THE ORDER OF

5,000.00

IN YOUR CURRENCY

LIVE THE EXPERIENCE IN THE NOW

FOR

SIGN NAME HERE

ASK, BELIEVE,
RECEIVE

ASK

What are ready to take the vibrational journey to?
By asking for this desire it means you are creating a gap and your job is to close it.

BELIEVE/SOURCE

THE MINUTE YOU ASK, IT IS DONE VIBRATIONALLY COMPLETE AND 99.99% DONE PHYSICALLY

RECEIVE:

Create a momentum in belief by feeling it is yours for 20 second, snap shots at a time. Focusing only on feeling not image.

If you hold an emotion as the desire. You no longer are creating an impossibility. The shift from in the future having the desire becomes felt in the present moment, and you will notice the tension has left the solar plexus as you do this.
At this moment you are able to isolate the components of the desire even without having the desire. You become expectant, Being expectant is a very high frequency, and it is one step away from the manifestation to occur.

What do you feel ready to change in your life.
By asking you are now saying "I will deliberately start creating this climate to close the gap.
I am aware of my part in how long the manifestation will take.

_____

_____

_____

_____

_____

Source has now become this vibrationally.
Your work is to create a mimicking or matching vibration.

Faith is created by reaching for the feeling and trusting the manifestation will follow.
Start now creating the feeling it is done by using small 20-second Virtual Realities while conjuring the emotions.
The idea is to preserve the focus that feels good longer, so you can match the frequency and enjoy the pleasures it provides in feelings.
Always leave the imagination
play through, if you feel anything but enjoyment.

POSITIVE ASPECTS

Appreciation is one of the highest vibrations you can use to shift how you are feeling.
It will build momentum fast and create an overall positive experience.
Even when you are in the worst of moods, if you focus on the parts that
you are appreciative for you will begin to start a new point of attraction.

I APPRECIATE YOU!
PERSON
NAME: *WHY?*

_____
_____
_____
_____
_____

I APPRECIATE THE
BEAUTY FOUND HERE.
PLACE: *WHY?*

_____
_____
_____
_____

I APPRECIATE THE
BEAUTY FOUND HERE.
PLACE: *WHY?*

_____
_____
_____
_____

I APPRECIATE YOU!
PERSON
NAME: *WHY?*

_____
_____
_____
_____

I APPRECIATE HAVING
ACCESS TO THIS.
THING: *WHY?*

_____
_____
_____
_____

WHAT I LOVE ABOUT
THE WEATHER: *WHY?*

_____
_____
_____
_____

I APPRECIATE YOU!
PERSON
NAME: *WHY?*

_____
_____
_____

I APPRECIATE HAVING
ACCESS TO THIS.
THING: *WHY?*

_____
_____
_____

WHAT I LOVE ABOUT..
                         WHY?

_____
_____
_____

POSITIVE
ASPECTS

Focus on anything and everything. Saying "thank you"
Creates more things to be thankful for.

I AM THANKFUL FOR: *WHY?*

_____
_____
_____
_____
_____

I AM THANKFUL FOR: *WHY?*

_____
_____
_____
_____
_____

I AM THANKFUL FOR: *WHY?*

_____
_____
_____
_____
_____

I AM THANKFUL FOR: *WHY?*

_____
_____
_____
_____
_____

I AM THANKFUL FOR: *WHY?*

_____
_____
_____
_____
_____

I AM THANKFUL FOR: *WHY?*

_____
_____
_____
_____
_____

I AM THANKFUL FOR: *WHY?*

_____
_____
_____
_____

I AM THANKFUL FOR: *WHY?*

_____
_____
_____
_____

I AM THANKFUL FOR: *WHY?*

_____
_____
_____
_____

FOODS
yum! WHAT MY BODY ENJOYED TODAY

_____
_____
_____
_____
_____

WATER INTAKE ✓
AM I HYDRATED?

GET PHYSICAL
WHAT MOVEMENT DID MY BODY ENJOY TODAY

_____
_____
_____
_____

MEDITATION
SPEND 15 MINS FOCUSING ON REPETITIVE SOUND. THE MORE BORING IT IS THE BETTER.

A TO Z
WRITE WORDS FROM A TO Z FEELING FOR THEM AS YOU WRITE THEM MAKE UP WORDS IF YOU CANT THINK OF ONE.

A_____ B_____ C_____ D_____

E_____ F_____ G_____ H_____

I_____ J_____ K_____ L_____

M_____ N_____ O_____ P_____

Q_____ R_____ S_____ T_____

U_____ V_____ W_____ X_____

Y_____ Z_____

Am I match ____
If I am feeling ease and comfort in this moment then I am.
I will sit in the feeling of satisfaction at focusing on these emotions right now.

1 SIT FOR ONE MINUTE BREATHING

Focus on holding a smile while taking in long and deep breaths in and slowly letting them out. Relax your body and feel the comfort of where you sit.

2 REMIND YOURSELF HOW IMPORTANT IT IS TO FEEL GOOD.

Today, nothing is more important then I feel good.

3
Write that here:

_____
_____
_____
_____
_____
_____

4
Close your eyes and see yourself aligning with source, blending into one. Thank this constant focus upon you.

5
NOTICE HOW THE SUN CAME UP AND THINGS ARE ALWAYS IN MOTION.

6
Feel and give thanks for the abundance of well-being all around. For a full minute.

What 4 things would I like to turn over to the Universe to take care of for me today?

1._____
2._____
3._____
4._____

When you stop looking for the desired manifestation, you learn that the feeling grows and carries you to the destination.

Write what things you intend to do today and how you intend to feel as you accomplish these things.

1._____Feeling_____
2._____Feeling_____
3._____Feeling_____
4._____Feeling_____

I look forward to enjoying a productive and fun day.

Pick one of these emotions you would like to use
as today's intended feeling.
Ease, Relaxed, Comfort
Write this feeling here:_____
Now say to yourself...

1.
MY INTENTION IS TO REMIND MYSELF MANY TIMES TODAY...

FOCUSING ON THIS FEELING OF_____
IS MY REAL JOB FOR THE DAY.

2.
MY CURRENT CONDITIONS ARE IRRELEVANT BECAUSE...

I'M CREATING AN ENVIRONMENT THAT IS CAUSING THEM TO CHANGE.

3.
NO MORE SNAPSHOTS OF WHAT IS OR FEELING HELPLESS.

TODAY, I AM GOING TO USE THIS EMOTION AS MY BASE FEELING THAT WILL EFFECT FUTURE OUTCOMES.

Close your eyes again and reach for this intended feeing in place of the feeling of current reality. Notice the softening of your body as you aligning with source.

Write your chosen daily focused emotion reaching for the feeling.

_____ _____ _____
_____ _____ _____
_____ _____ _____
_____ _____ _____

ASK YOURSELF MANY TIMES TODAY
"Is this the attracting vibration, I want the universe to respond to?"
If not, for the count of 10 long breaths in and
slowly letting them out.
Say and feel your chosen emotion in appreciation for the feeling.
It self-creates without any evidence needed.

Write 3 things you would be interested in seeing that just for fun but you are not worried about when.

_____
_____
_____

Let the universe show you these things in playful and exciting ways.

A THOUGHT REACHES A COMBUSTION POINT AT 16 SECONDS.

VIBRATIONAL CASH

A FULL 68 SECONDS ARE EQUIVALENT TO 2 MILLION MAN-HOURS.

Spend Your Vibrational Cash on one thing a day. If wanting a big ticket item slowly pay it off. This will make it more real for you.

The longer you spend feeling like the recipient of this desire the closer you are in being a match to it.

Focus on how it feels to buy this desire and the satisfaction attached within having it. Write about that satisfaction.

Close your eyes again and reach for the first thing that pops into your mind. No matter what the price tag is, big and small creations are all the same. Learn to start treating them all equal.

VIBRATIONALCASH

DATE _____

PAY TO THE ORDER OF

5,000.00

IN YOUR CURRENCY

_____

LIVE THE EXPERIENCE IN THE NOW

FOR _____

SIGN NAME HERE

_____
_____
_____
_____
_____
_____
_____
_____
_____

ASK, BELIEVE,
RECEIVE

ASK

What are ready to take the vibrational journey to?
By asking for this desire it means you are creating a gap and your job is to close it.

BELIEVE/SOURCE

THE MINUTE YOU ASK, IT IS DONE VIBRATIONALLY COMPLETE AND 99.99% DONE PHYSICALLY

RECEIVE:

Create a momentum in belief by feeling it is yours for 20 second, snap shots at a time. Focusing only on feeling not image.

If you hold an emotion as the desire. You no longer are creating an impossibility. The shift from in the future having the desire becomes felt in the present moment, and you will notice the tension has left the solar plexus as you do this.
At this moment you are able to isolate the components of the desire even without having the desire. You become expectant, Being expectant is a very high frequency, and it is one step away from the manifestation to occur.

What do you feel ready to change in your life.
By asking you are now saying "I will deliberately start creating this climate to close the gap.
I am aware of my part in how long the manifestation will take.

_____
_____
_____
_____
_____

Source has now become this vibrationally.
Your work is to create a mimicking or matching vibration.

Faith is created by reaching for the feeling and trusting the manifestation will follow.
Start now creating the feeling it is done by using small 20-second Virtual Realities while conjuring the emotions.
The idea is to preserve the focus that feels good longer, so you can match the frequency and enjoy the pleasures it provides in feelings.
Always leave the imagination play through, if you feel anything but enjoyment.

POSITIVE ASPECTS

Appreciation is one of the highest vibrations you can use to shift how you are feeling.
It will build momentum fast and create an overall positive experience.
Even when you are in the worst of moods, if you focus on the parts that
you are appreciative for you will begin to start a new point of attraction.

I APPRECIATE YOU!
PERSON
NAME: *WHY?*

_____
_____
_____
_____
_____

I APPRECIATE THE
BEAUTY FOUND HERE.
PLACE: *WHY?*

_____
_____
_____
_____
_____

I APPRECIATE THE
BEAUTY FOUND HERE.
PLACE: *WHY?*

_____
_____
_____
_____
_____

I APPRECIATE YOU!
PERSON
NAME: *WHY?*

_____
_____
_____
_____
_____

I APPRECIATE HAVING
ACCESS TO THIS.
THING: *WHY?*

_____
_____
_____
_____
_____

WHAT I LOVE ABOUT
THE WEATHER: *WHY?*

_____
_____
_____
_____
_____

I APPRECIATE YOU!
PERSON
NAME: *WHY?*

_____
_____
_____
_____
_____

I APPRECIATE HAVING
ACCESS TO THIS.
THING: *WHY?*

_____
_____
_____
_____
_____

WHAT I LOVE ABOUT..
              WHY?

_____
_____
_____
_____
_____

POSITIVE
ASPECTS

Focus on anything and everything. Saying "thank you"
Creates more things to be thankful for.

I AM THANKFUL FOR: *WHY?*

_____
_____
_____
_____
_____

I AM THANKFUL FOR: *WHY?*

_____
_____
_____
_____
_____

I AM THANKFUL FOR: *WHY?*

_____
_____
_____
_____
_____

I AM THANKFUL FOR: *WHY?*

_____
_____
_____
_____
_____

I AM THANKFUL FOR: *WHY?*

_____
_____
_____
_____
_____

I AM THANKFUL FOR: *WHY?*

_____
_____
_____
_____
_____

I AM THANKFUL FOR: *WHY?*

_____
_____
_____
_____

I AM THANKFUL FOR: *WHY?*

_____
_____
_____
_____

I AM THANKFUL FOR: *WHY?*

_____
_____
_____
_____

FOODS
yum! WHAT MY BODY ENJOYED TODAY

_____

_____

_____

_____

_____

_____

WATER INTAKE
AM I HYDRATED?

GET PHYSICAL
WHAT MOVEMENT DID MY BODY ENJOY TODAY

_____

_____

_____

_____

_____

MEDITATION

SPEND 15 MINS FOCUSING ON REPETITIVE SOUND. THE MORE BORING IT IS THE BETTER.

A TO Z

WRITE WORDS FROM A TO Z FEELING FOR THEM AS YOU WRITE THEM MAKE UP WORDS IF YOU CANT THINK OF ONE.

A_____ B_____ C_____ D_____

E_____ F_____ G_____ H_____

I_____ J_____ K_____ L_____

M_____ N_____ O_____ P_____

Q_____ R_____ S_____ T_____

U_____ V_____ W_____ X_____

Y_____ Z_____

Am I match ____
If I am feeling ease and comfort in this moment then I am.
I will sit in the feeling of satisfaction at focusing on these emotions right now.

1 SIT FOR ONE MINUTE BREATHING

Focus on holding a smile while taking in long and deep breaths in and slowly letting them out. Relax your body and feel the comfort of where you sit.

2 REMIND YOURSELF HOW IMPORTANT IT IS TO FEEL GOOD.

Today, nothing is more important then I feel good.

3

Write that here:

_____

_____

_____

_____

_____

_____

_____

4

Close your eyes and see yourself aligning with source, blending into one.
Thank this constant focus upon you.

5

NOTICE HOW THE SUN CAME UP AND THINGS ARE ALWAYS IN MOTION.

6

Feel and give thanks for the abundance of well-being all around.
For a full minute.

What 4 things would I like to turn over to the Universe to take care of for me today?

1._____

2._____

3._____

4._____

When you stop looking for the desired manifestation, you learn that the feeling grows and carries you to the destination.

Write what things you intend to do today and how you intend to feel as you accomplish these things.

1._____Feeling_____

2._____Feeling_____

3._____Feeling_____

4._____Feeling_____

I look forward to enjoying a productive and fun day.

Pick one of these emotions you would like to use
as today's intended feeling.
Ease, Relaxed, Comfort
Write this feeling here:_____
Now say to yourself...

1.
MY INTENTION IS TO REMIND MYSELF MANY TIMES TODAY...

FOCUSING ON THIS FEELING OF_____ IS MY REAL JOB FOR THE DAY.

2.
MY CURRENT CONDITIONS ARE IRRELEVANT BECAUSE...

I'M CREATING AN ENVIRONMENT THAT IS CAUSING THEM TO CHANGE.

3.
NO MORE SNAPSHOTS OF WHAT IS OR FEELING HELPLESS.

TODAY, I AM GOING TO USE THIS EMOTION AS MY BASE FEELING THAT WILL EFFECT FUTURE OUTCOMES.

Close your eyes again and reach for this intended feeing in place of the feeling of current reality. Notice the softening of your body as you aligning with source.

Write your chosen daily focused emotion reaching for the feeling.

_____ _____ _____
_____ _____ _____
_____ _____ _____
_____ _____ _____

ASK YOURSELF MANY TIMES TODAY
"Is this the attracting vibration, I want the universe to respond to?"
If not, for the count of 10 long breaths in and
slowly letting them out.
Say and feel your chosen emotion in appreciation for the feeling.
It self-creates without any evidence needed.

Write 3 things you would be interested in seeing that just for fun but you are not worried about when.

_____
_____
_____

Let the universe show you these things in playful and exciting ways.

A THOUGHT REACHES A COMBUSTION POINT AT 16 SECONDS.

VIBRATIONAL CASH

A FULL 68 SECONDS ARE EQUIVALENT TO 2 MILLION MAN-HOURS.

Spend Your Vibrational Cash on one thing a day. If wanting a big ticket item slowly pay it off. This will make it more real for you.

The longer you spend feeling like the recipient of this desire the closer you are in being a match to it.

Focus on how it feels to buy this desire and the satisfaction attached within having it. Write about that satisfaction.

Close your eyes again and reach for the first thing that pops into your mind. No matter what the price tag is, big and small creations are all the same. Learn to start treating them all equal.

VibrationalCash

DATE _____

PAY TO THE ORDER OF _____

5,000.00

IN YOUR CURRENCY

_____

LIVE THE EXPERIENCE IN THE NOW

FOR _____

_____
SIGN NAME HERE

_____
_____
_____
_____
_____
_____
_____
_____
_____
_____

ASK, BELIEVE,
RECEIVE

ASK

What are ready to take the vibrational journey to?
By asking for this desire it means you are creating a gap and your job is to close it.

BELIEVE/SOURCE

THE MINUTE YOU ASK, IT IS DONE VIBRATIONALLY COMPLETE AND 99.99% DONE PHYSICALLY

RECEIVE:

Create a momentum in belief by feeling it is yours for 20 second, snap shots at a time. Focusing only on feeling not image.

If you hold an emotion as the desire. You no longer are creating an impossibility. The shift from in the future having the desire becomes felt in the present moment, and you will notice the tension has left the solar plexus as you do this.
At this moment you are able to isolate the components of the desire even without having the desire. You become expectant, Being expectant is a very high frequency, and it is one step away from the manifestation to occur.

◄──►

What do you feel ready to change in your life.
By asking you are now saying "I will deliberately start creating this climate to close the gap.
I am aware of my part in how long the manifestation will take.

_____
_____
_____
_____
_____

Source has now become this vibrationally.
Your work is to create a mimicking or matching vibration.

Faith is created by reaching for the feeling and trusting the manifestation will follow.
Start now creating the feeling it is done by using small 20-second Virtual Realities while conjuring the emotions.
The idea is to preserve the focus that feels good longer, so you can match the frequency and enjoy the pleasures it provides in feelings.
Always leave the imagination play through, if you feel anything but enjoyment.

POSITIVE ASPECTS

Appreciation is one of the highest vibrations you can use to shift how you are feeling.
It will build momentum fast and create an overall positive experience.
Even when you are in the worst of moods, if you focus on the parts that
you are appreciative for you will begin to start a new point of attraction.

I APPRECIATE YOU!
PERSON
NAME: *WHY?*

_____
_____
_____
_____
_____

**I APPRECIATE THE
BEAUTY FOUND HERE.**
PLACE: *WHY?*

_____
_____
_____
_____
_____

**I APPRECIATE THE
BEAUTY FOUND HERE.**
PLACE: *WHY?*

_____
_____
_____
_____
_____

I APPRECIATE YOU!
PERSON
NAME: *WHY?*

_____
_____
_____
_____

**I APPRECIATE HAVING
ACCESS TO THIS.**
THING: *WHY?*

_____
_____
_____
_____

**WHAT I LOVE ABOUT
THE WEATHER:** *WHY?*

_____
_____
_____
_____

I APPRECIATE YOU!
PERSON
NAME: *WHY?*

_____
_____
_____
_____

**I APPRECIATE HAVING
ACCESS TO THIS.**
THING: *WHY?*

_____
_____
_____
_____

WHAT I LOVE ABOUT.. *WHY?*

_____
_____
_____
_____

POSITIVE
ASPECTS

Focus on anything and everything. Saying "thank you"
Creates more things to be thankful for.

I AM THANKFUL FOR: _WHY?_

_____
_____
_____
_____
_____

I AM THANKFUL FOR: _WHY?_

_____
_____
_____
_____
_____

I AM THANKFUL FOR: _WHY?_

_____
_____
_____
_____
_____

I AM THANKFUL FOR: _WHY?_

_____
_____
_____
_____
_____

I AM THANKFUL FOR: _WHY?_

_____
_____
_____
_____
_____

I AM THANKFUL FOR: _WHY?_

_____
_____
_____
_____
_____

I AM THANKFUL FOR: _WHY?_

_____
_____
_____
_____

I AM THANKFUL FOR: _WHY?_

_____
_____
_____
_____

I AM THANKFUL FOR: _WHY?_

_____
_____
_____
_____

FOODS
yum! WHAT MY BODY ENJOYED TODAY

_____
_____
_____
_____
_____
_____

WATER INTAKE ✓
AM I HYDRATED?

GET PHYSICAL
WHAT MOVEMENT DID MY BODY ENJOY TODAY

_____
_____
_____
_____
_____

MEDITATION

SPEND 15 MINS FOCUSING ON REPETITIVE SOUND. THE MORE BORING IT IS THE BETTER.

A TO Z

WRITE WORDS FROM A TO Z FEELING FOR THEM AS YOU WRITE THEM MAKE UP WORDS IF YOU CANT THINK OF ONE.

A_____ B_____ C_____ D_____

E_____ F_____ G_____ H_____

I_____ J_____ K_____ L_____

M_____ N_____ O_____ P_____

Q_____ R_____ S_____ T_____

U_____ V_____ W_____ X_____

Y_____ Z_____

Am I match ____
If I am feeling ease and comfort in this moment then I am.
I will sit in the feeling of satisfaction at focusing on these emotions right now.

1 SIT FOR ONE MINUTE BREATHING

Focus on holding a smile while taking in long and deep breaths in and slowly letting them out. Relax your body and feel the comfort of where you sit.

2 REMIND YOURSELF HOW IMPORTANT IT IS TO FEEL GOOD.

Today, nothing is more important then I feel good.

3

Write that here:

_____

_____

_____

_____

_____

_____

_____

5

NOTICE HOW THE SUN CAME UP AND THINGS ARE ALWAYS IN MOTION.

4

Close your eyes and see yourself aligning with source, blending into one.
Thank this constant focus upon you.

6

Feel and give thanks for the abundance of well-being all around.
For a full minute.

What 4 things would I like to turn over to the Universe to take care of for me today?

1._____

2._____

3._____

4._____

When you stop looking for the desired manifestation, you learn that the feeling grows and carries you to the destination.

Write what things you intend to do today and how you intend to feel as you accomplish these things.

1._____Feeling_____

2._____Feeling_____

3._____Feeling_____

4._____Feeling_____

I look forward to enjoying a productive and fun day.

Pick one of these emotions you would like to use
as today's intended feeling.
Ease, Relaxed, Comfort
Write this feeling here:_____
Now say to yourself...

1.
MY INTENTION IS TO REMIND MYSELF MANY TIMES TODAY...

FOCUSING ON THIS FEELING OF_____ IS MY REAL JOB FOR THE DAY.

2.
MY CURRENT CONDITIONS ARE IRRELEVANT BECAUSE...

I'M CREATING AN ENVIRONMENT THAT IS CAUSING THEM TO CHANGE.

3.
NO MORE SNAPSHOTS OF WHAT IS OR FEELING HELPLESS.

TODAY, I AM GOING TO USE THIS EMOTION AS MY BASE FEELING THAT WILL EFFECT FUTURE OUTCOMES.

Close your eyes again and reach for this intended feeing in
place of the feeling of current reality. Notice the softening
of your body as you aligning with source.

Write your chosen daily focused emotion reaching
for the feeling.

_____ _____ _____
_____ _____ _____
_____ _____ _____
_____ _____ _____

ASK YOURSELF MANY TIMES TODAY
"Is this the attracting vibration, I want the universe to respond to?"
If not, for the count of 10 long breaths in and
slowly letting them out.
Say and feel your chosen emotion in appreciation for the feeling.
It self-creates without any evidence needed.

Write 3 things you would be interested in seeing that just for fun but
you are not worried about when.

_____
_____
_____

Let the universe show you these things in playful and exciting ways.

A THOUGHT REACHES A COMBUSTION POINT AT 16 SECONDS.

VIBRATIONAL CASH

A FULL 68 SECONDS ARE EQUIVALENT TO 2 MILLION MAN-HOURS.

Spend Your Vibrational Cash on one thing a day. If wanting a big ticket item slowly pay it off. This will make it more real for you.

The longer you spend feeling like the recipient of this desire the closer you are in being a match to it.

Focus on how it feels to buy this desire and the satisfaction attached within having it. Write about that satisfaction.

Close your eyes again and reach for the first thing that pops into your mind. No matter what the price tag is, big and small creations are all the same. Learn to start treating them all equal.

VIBRATIONAL CASH

PAY TO THE ORDER OF

DATE

5,000.00

IN YOUR CURRENCY

LIVE THE EXPERIENCE IN THE NOW

FOR

SIGN NAME HERE

ASK, BELIEVE,
RECEIVE

ASK

What are ready to take the vibrational journey to?
By asking for this desire it means you are creating a gap and your job is to close it.

BELIEVE/SOURCE

THE MINUTE YOU ASK, IT IS DONE VIBRATIONALLY COMPLETE AND 99.99% DONE PHYSICALLY

RECEIVE:

Create a momentum in belief by feeling it is yours for 20 second, snap shots at a time. Focusing only on feeling not image.

If you hold an emotion as the desire. You no longer are creating an impossibility. The shift from in the future having the desire becomes felt in the present moment, and you will notice the tension has left the solar plexus as you do this.
At this moment you are able to isolate the components of the desire even without having the desire. You become expectant, Being expectant is a very high frequency, and it is one step away from the manifestation to occur.

⬅——————————————————➡

What do you feel ready to change in your life.
By asking you are now saying "I will deliberately start creating this climate to close the gap. I am aware of my part in how long the manifestation will take.

_____
_____
_____
_____
_____

Source has now become this vibrationally.
Your work is to create a mimicking or matching vibration.

Faith is created by reaching for the feeling and trusting the manifestation will follow.
Start now creating the feeling it is done by using small 20-second Virtual Realities while conjuring the emotions.
The idea is to preserve the focus that feels good longer, so you can match the frequency and enjoy the pleasures it provides in feelings.
Always leave the imagination play through, if you feel anything but enjoyment.

POSITIVE ASPECTS

Appreciation is one of the highest vibrations you can use to shift how you are feeling.
It will build momentum fast and create an overall positive experience.
Even when you are in the worst of moods, if you focus on the parts that
you are appreciative for you will begin to start a new point of attraction.

I APPRECIATE YOU!
PERSON
NAME: *WHY?*

_____
_____
_____
_____
_____

I APPRECIATE THE
BEAUTY FOUND HERE.
PLACE: *WHY?*

_____
_____
_____
_____
_____

I APPRECIATE THE
BEAUTY FOUND HERE.
PLACE: *WHY?*

_____
_____
_____
_____
_____

I APPRECIATE YOU!
PERSON
NAME: *WHY?*

_____
_____
_____
_____

I APPRECIATE HAVING
ACCESS TO THIS.
THING: *WHY?*

_____
_____
_____
_____

WHAT I LOVE ABOUT
THE WEATHER: *WHY?*

_____
_____
_____
_____

I APPRECIATE YOU!
PERSON
NAME: *WHY?*

_____
_____
_____
_____

I APPRECIATE HAVING
ACCESS TO THIS.
THING: *WHY?*

_____
_____
_____
_____

WHAT I LOVE ABOUT..
                         WHY?

_____
_____
_____
_____

POSITIVE
ASPECTS

Focus on anything and everything. Saying "thank you"
Creates more things to be thankful for.

I AM THANKFUL FOR:	WHY?

I AM THANKFUL FOR:	WHY?

I AM THANKFUL FOR:	WHY?

I AM THANKFUL FOR:	WHY?

I AM THANKFUL FOR:	WHY?

I AM THANKFUL FOR:	WHY?

I AM THANKFUL FOR:	WHY?

I AM THANKFUL FOR:	WHY?

I AM THANKFUL FOR:	WHY?

FOODS

yum! **WHAT MY BODY ENJOYED TODAY**

_____
_____
_____
_____
_____
_____

WATER INTAKE

AM I HYDRATED? ✓

GET PHYSICAL

WHAT MOVEMENT DID MY BODY ENJOY TODAY

_____
_____
_____
_____

MEDITATION

SPEND 15 MINS FOCUSING ON REPETITIVE SOUND. THE MORE BORING IT IS THE BETTER.

A TO Z

WRITE WORDS FROM A TO Z FEELING FOR THEM AS YOU WRITE THEM MAKE UP WORDS IF YOU CANT THINK OF ONE.

A_____ B_____ C_____ D_____

E_____ F_____ G_____ H_____

I_____ J_____ K_____ L_____

M_____ N_____ O_____ P_____

Q_____ R_____ S_____ T_____

U_____ V_____ W_____ X_____

Y_____ Z_____

Am I match _____
If I am feeling ease and comfort in this moment then I am.
I will sit in the feeling of satisfaction at focusing on these emotions right now.

1 SIT FOR ONE MINUTE BREATHING

Focus on holding a smile while taking in long and deep breaths in and slowly letting them out. Relax your body and feel the comfort of where you sit.

2 REMIND YOURSELF HOW IMPORTANT IT IS TO FEEL GOOD.

Today, nothing is more important then I feel good.

3
Write that here:

_____

_____

_____

_____

_____

_____

_____

5
NOTICE HOW THE SUN CAME UP AND THINGS ARE ALWAYS IN MOTION.

4
Close your eyes and see yourself aligning with source, blending into one.
Thank this constant focus upon you.

6
Feel and give thanks for the abundance of well-being all around.
For a full minute.

What 4 things would I like to turn over to the Universe
to take care of for me today?

1._____

2._____

3._____

4._____

When you stop looking for the desired manifestation,
you learn that the feeling grows and carries you to the destination.

Write what things you intend to do today
and how you intend to feel as you accomplish these things.

1._____Feeling_____

2._____Feeling_____

3._____Feeling_____

4._____Feeling_____

I look forward to enjoying a productive and fun day.

Pick one of these emotions you would like to use
as today's intended feeling.
Ease, Relaxed, Comfort
Write this feeling here:_____
Now say to yourself...

1.
MY INTENTION IS TO REMIND MYSELF MANY TIMES TODAY...

FOCUSING ON THIS FEELING OF_____ IS MY REAL JOB FOR THE DAY.

2.
MY CURRENT CONDITIONS ARE IRRELEVANT BECAUSE...

I'M CREATING AN ENVIRONMENT THAT IS CAUSING THEM TO CHANGE.

3.
NO MORE SNAPSHOTS OF WHAT IS OR FEELING HELPLESS.

TODAY, I AM GOING TO USE THIS EMOTION AS MY BASE FEELING THAT WILL EFFECT FUTURE OUTCOMES.

Close your eyes again and reach for this intended feeing in place of the feeling of current reality. Notice the softening of your body as you aligning with source.

Write your chosen daily focused emotion reaching for the feeling.

_____ _____ _____
_____ _____ _____
_____ _____ _____
_____ _____ _____

ASK YOURSELF MANY TIMES TODAY
"Is this the attracting vibration, I want the universe to respond to?"
If not, for the count of 10 long breaths in and
slowly letting them out.
Say and feel your chosen emotion in appreciation for the feeling.
It self-creates without any evidence needed.

Write 3 things you would be interested in seeing that just for fun but you are not worried about when.

_____
_____
_____

Let the universe show you these things in playful and exciting ways.

A THOUGHT REACHES A COMBUSTION POINT AT 16 SECONDS.

VIBRATIONAL
CASH

A FULL 68 SECONDS ARE EQUIVALENT TO 2 MILLION MAN-HOURS.

Spend Your Vibrational Cash on one thing a day. If wanting a big ticket item slowly pay it off. This will make it more real for you.

The longer you spend feeling like the recipient of this desire the closer you are in being a match to it.

Focus on how it feels to buy this desire and the satisfaction attached within having it. Write about that satisfaction.

Close your eyes again and reach for the first thing that pops into your mind. No matter what the price tag is, big and small creations are all the same. Learn to start treating them all equal.

VIBRATIONALCASH

DATE _____

PAY TO THE ORDER OF

5,000.00

IN YOUR CURRENCY

LIVE THE EXPERIENCE IN THE NOW

FOR _____

SIGN NAME HERE

_____
_____
_____
_____
_____
_____
_____
_____
_____
_____

ASK, BELIEVE,
RECEIVE

ASK

What are ready to take the vibrational journey to?
By asking for this desire it means you are creating a gap and your job is to close it.

BELIEVE/SOURCE

THE MINUTE YOU ASK, IT IS DONE VIBRATIONALLY COMPLETE AND 99.99% DONE PHYSICALLY

RECEIVE:

Create a momentum in belief by feeling it is yours for 20 second, snap shots at a time. Focusing only on feeling not image.

If you hold an emotion as the desire. You no longer are creating an impossibility. The shift from in the future having the desire becomes felt in the present moment, and you will notice the tension has left the solar plexus as you do this.
At this moment you are able to isolate the components of the desire even without having the desire. You become expectant, Being expectant is a very high frequency, and it is one step away from the manifestation to occur.

What do you feel ready to change in your life.
By asking you are now saying "I will deliberately start creating this climate to close the gap.
I am aware of my part in how long the manifestation will take.

_____
_____
_____
_____
_____

Source has now become this vibrationally.
Your work is to create a mimicking or matching vibration.

Faith is created by reaching for the feeling and trusting the manifestation will follow.
Start now creating the feeling it is done by using small 20-second Virtual Realities while conjuring the emotions.
The idea is to preserve the focus that feels good longer, so you can match the frequency and enjoy the pleasures it provides in feelings.
Always leave the imagination
play through, if you feel anything but enjoyment.

POSITIVE ASPECTS

Appreciation is one of the highest vibrations you can use to shift how you are feeling.
It will build momentum fast and create an overall positive experience.
Even when you are in the worst of moods, if you focus on the parts that
you are appreciative for you will begin to start a new point of attraction.

I APPRECIATE YOU!
PERSON
NAME: *WHY?*

_____
_____
_____
_____
_____

I APPRECIATE THE
BEAUTY FOUND HERE.
PLACE: *WHY?*

_____
_____
_____
_____
_____

I APPRECIATE THE
BEAUTY FOUND HERE.
PLACE: *WHY?*

_____
_____
_____
_____
_____

I APPRECIATE YOU!
PERSON
NAME: *WHY?*

_____
_____
_____
_____

I APPRECIATE HAVING
ACCESS TO THIS.
THING: *WHY?*

_____
_____
_____
_____

WHAT I LOVE ABOUT
THE WEATHER: *WHY?*

_____
_____
_____
_____

I APPRECIATE YOU!
PERSON
NAME: *WHY?*

_____
_____
_____
_____

I APPRECIATE HAVING
ACCESS TO THIS.
THING: *WHY?*

_____
_____
_____
_____

WHAT I LOVE ABOUT..
WHY?

_____
_____
_____
_____

POSITIVE
ASPECTS

Focus on anything and everything. Saying "thank you"
Creates more things to be thankful for.

I AM THANKFUL FOR: *WHY?*

_____
_____
_____
_____
_____

I AM THANKFUL FOR: *WHY?*

_____
_____
_____
_____
_____

I AM THANKFUL FOR: *WHY?*

_____
_____
_____
_____
_____

I AM THANKFUL FOR: *WHY?*

_____
_____
_____
_____
_____

I AM THANKFUL FOR: *WHY?*

_____
_____
_____
_____
_____

I AM THANKFUL FOR: *WHY?*

_____
_____
_____
_____
_____

I AM THANKFUL FOR: *WHY?*

_____
_____
_____
_____
_____

I AM THANKFUL FOR: *WHY?*

_____
_____
_____
_____
_____

I AM THANKFUL FOR: *WHY?*

_____
_____
_____
_____
_____

FOODS

yum! WHAT MY BODY ENJOYED TODAY

_____
_____
_____
_____
_____
_____

WATER INTAKE ✓

AM I HYDRATED?

GET PHYSICAL

WHAT MOVEMENT DID MY BODY ENJOY TODAY

_____
_____
_____
_____

MEDITATION

SPEND 15 MINS FOCUSING ON REPETITIVE SOUND. THE MORE BORING IT IS THE BETTER.

A TO Z

WRITE WORDS FROM A TO Z FEELING FOR THEM AS YOU WRITE THEM MAKE UP WORDS IF YOU CANT THINK OF ONE.

A_____ B_____ C_____ D_____

E_____ F_____ G_____ H_____

I_____ J_____ K_____ L_____

M_____ N_____ O_____ P_____

Q_____ R_____ S_____ T_____

U_____ V_____ W_____ X_____

Y_____ Z_____

Am I match _____
If I am feeling ease and comfort in this moment then I am.
I will sit in the feeling of satisfaction at focusing on these emotions right now.

1 SIT FOR ONE MINUTE BREATHING

Focus on holding a smile while taking in long and deep breaths in and slowly letting them out. Relax your body and feel the comfort of where you sit.

2 REMIND YOURSELF HOW IMPORTANT IT IS TO FEEL GOOD.

Today, nothing is more important then I feel good.

3

Write that here:

_____
_____
_____
_____
_____
_____
_____

4

Close your eyes and see yourself aligning with source, blending into one.
Thank this constant focus upon you.

5

NOTICE HOW THE SUN CAME UP AND THINGS ARE ALWAYS IN MOTION.

6

Feel and give thanks for the abundance of well-being all around.
For a full minute.

What 4 things would I like to turn over to the Universe to take care of for me today?

1._____
2._____
3._____
4._____

When you stop looking for the desired manifestation, you learn that the feeling grows and carries you to the destination.

Write what things you intend to do today and how you intend to feel as you accomplish these things.

1._____Feeling_____
2._____Feeling_____
3._____Feeling_____
4._____Feeling_____

I look forward to enjoying a productive and fun day.

Pick one of these emotions you would like to use
as today's intended feeling.
Ease, Relaxed, Comfort
Write this feeling here:_____
Now say to yourself...

**1.
MY INTENTION IS TO
REMIND MYSELF
MANY TIMES
TODAY...**

FOCUSING ON THIS
FEELING OF_____
IS MY REAL
JOB FOR THE DAY.

**2.
MY CURRENT
CONDITIONS ARE
IRRELEVANT
BECAUSE...**

I'M CREATING AN
ENVIRONMENT THAT
IS CAUSING THEM TO
CHANGE.

**3.
NO MORE SNAPSHOTS
OF WHAT IS
OR FEELING HELPLESS.**

TODAY, I AM GOING
TO USE THIS EMOTION
AS MY BASE FEELING
THAT WILL EFFECT
FUTURE OUTCOMES.

Close your eyes again and reach for this intended feeing in
place of the feeling of current reality. Notice the softening
of your body as you aligning with source.

Write your chosen daily focused emotion reaching
for the feeling.

_____ _____ _____
_____ _____ _____
_____ _____ _____
_____ _____ _____

ASK YOURSELF MANY TIMES TODAY
"Is this the attracting vibration, I want the universe to respond to?"
If not, for the count of 10 long breaths in and
slowly letting them out.
Say and feel your chosen emotion in appreciation for the feeling.
It self-creates without any evidence needed.

Write 3 things you would be interested in seeing that just for fun but
you are not worried about when.

_____
_____
_____

Let the universe show you these things in playful and exciting ways.

VIBRATIONAL CASH

A THOUGHT REACHES A COMBUSTION POINT AT 16 SECONDS.

Spend Your Vibrational Cash on one thing a day. If wanting a big ticket item slowly pay it off. This will make it more real for you.

The longer you spend feeling like the recipient of this desire the closer you are in being a match to it.

A FULL 68 SECONDS ARE EQUIVALENT TO 2 MILLION MAN-HOURS.

Focus on how it feels to buy this desire and the satisfaction attached within having it. Write about that satisfaction.

Close your eyes again and reach for the first thing that pops into your mind. No matter what the price tag is, big and small creations are all the same. Learn to start treating them all equal.

VIBRATIONAL CASH

DATE _____

PAY TO THE ORDER OF

5,000.00

IN YOUR CURRENCY

_____

LIVE THE EXPERIENCE IN THE NOW

FOR _____

SIGN NAME HERE

_____
_____
_____
_____
_____
_____
_____
_____
_____

ASK, BELIEVE, RECEIVE

ASK

What are ready to take the vibrational journey to?
By asking for this desire it means you are creating a gap and your job is to close it.

BELIEVE/SOURCE

THE MINUTE YOU ASK, IT IS DONE VIBRATIONALLY COMPLETE AND 99.99% DONE PHYSICALLY

RECEIVE:

Create a momentum in belief by feeling it is yours for 20 second, snap shots at a time. Focusing only on feeling not image.

If you hold an emotion as the desire. You no longer are creating an impossibility. The shift from in the future having the desire becomes felt in the present moment, and you will notice the tension has left the solar plexus as you do this.
At this moment you are able to isolate the components of the desire even without having the desire. You become expectant, Being expectant is a very high frequency, and it is one step away from the manifestation to occur.

What do you feel ready to change in your life.
By asking you are now saying "I will deliberately start creating this climate to close the gap.
I am aware of my part in how long the manifestation will take.

_____
_____
_____
_____
_____

Source has now become this vibrationally.
Your work is to create a mimicking or matching vibration.

Faith is created by reaching for the feeling and trusting the manifestation will follow.
Start now creating the feeling it is done by using small 20-second Virtual Realities while conjuring the emotions.
The idea is to preserve the focus that feels good longer, so you can match the frequency and enjoy the pleasures it provides in feelings.
Always leave the imagination play through, if you feel anything but enjoyment.

POSITIVE ASPECTS

Appreciation is one of the highest vibrations you can use to shift how you are feeling.
It will build momentum fast and create an overall positive experience.
Even when you are in the worst of moods, if you focus on the parts that
you are appreciative for you will begin to start a new point of attraction.

I APPRECIATE YOU!
PERSON
NAME: *WHY?*

_____
_____
_____
_____
_____

I APPRECIATE THE
BEAUTY FOUND HERE.
PLACE: *WHY?*

_____
_____
_____
_____
_____

I APPRECIATE THE
BEAUTY FOUND HERE.
PLACE: *WHY?*

_____
_____
_____
_____
_____

I APPRECIATE YOU!
PERSON
NAME: *WHY?*

_____
_____
_____
_____
_____

I APPRECIATE HAVING
ACCESS TO THIS.
THING: *WHY?*

_____
_____
_____
_____
_____

WHAT I LOVE ABOUT
THE WEATHER: *WHY?*

_____
_____
_____
_____
_____

I APPRECIATE YOU!
PERSON
NAME: *WHY?*

_____
_____
_____
_____
_____

I APPRECIATE HAVING
ACCESS TO THIS.
THING: *WHY?*

_____
_____
_____
_____
_____

WHAT I LOVE ABOUT..
               WHY?

_____
_____
_____
_____
_____

POSITIVE
ASPECTS

Focus on anything and everything. Saying "thank you"
Creates more things to be thankful for.

I AM THANKFUL FOR: *WHY?*

_____
_____
_____
_____
_____

I AM THANKFUL FOR: *WHY?*

_____
_____
_____
_____
_____

I AM THANKFUL FOR: *WHY?*

_____
_____
_____
_____
_____

I AM THANKFUL FOR: *WHY?*

_____
_____
_____
_____
_____

I AM THANKFUL FOR: *WHY?*

_____
_____
_____
_____
_____

I AM THANKFUL FOR: *WHY?*

_____
_____
_____
_____
_____

I AM THANKFUL FOR: *WHY?*

_____
_____
_____
_____

I AM THANKFUL FOR: *WHY?*

_____
_____
_____
_____

I AM THANKFUL FOR: *WHY?*

_____
_____
_____
_____

FOODS

YUM! WHAT MY BODY ENJOYED TODAY

_____

_____

_____

_____

_____

_____

WATER INTAKE

AM I HYDRATED? ✓

GET PHYSICAL

WHAT MOVEMENT DID MY BODY ENJOY TODAY

_____

_____

_____

_____

_____

MEDITATION

SPEND 15 MINS FOCUSING ON REPETITIVE SOUND. THE MORE BORING IT IS THE BETTER.

A TO Z

WRITE WORDS FROM A TO Z FEELING FOR THEM AS YOU WRITE THEM MAKE UP WORDS IF YOU CANT THINK OF ONE.

A_____ B_____ C_____ D_____

E_____ F_____ G_____ H_____

I_____ J_____ K_____ L_____

M_____ N_____ O_____ P_____

Q_____ R_____ S_____ T_____

U_____ V_____ W_____ X_____

Y_____ Z_____

Am I match _____
If I am feeling ease and comfort in this moment then I am.
I will sit in the feeling of satisfaction at focusing on these emotions right now.

1 SIT FOR ONE MINUTE BREATHING

Focus on holding a smile while taking in long and deep breaths in and slowly letting them out. Relax your body and feel the comfort of where you sit.

2 REMIND YOURSELF HOW IMPORTANT IT IS TO FEEL GOOD.

Today, nothing is more important then I feel good.

3

Write that here:

_____

_____

_____

_____

_____

_____

_____

5

NOTICE HOW THE SUN CAME UP AND THINGS ARE ALWAYS IN MOTION.

4

Close your eyes and see yourself aligning with source, blending into one.
Thank this constant focus upon you.

6

Feel and give thanks for the abundance of well-being all around.
For a full minute.

What 4 things would I like to turn over to the Universe to take care of for me today?

1._____
2._____
3._____
4._____

When you stop looking for the desired manifestation, you learn that the feeling grows and carries you to the destination.

Write what things you intend to do today and how you intend to feel as you accomplish these things.

1._____Feeling_____
2._____Feeling_____
3._____Feeling_____
4._____Feeling_____

I look forward to enjoying a productive and fun day.

Pick one of these emotions you would like to use
as today's intended feeling.
Ease, Relaxed, Comfort
Write this feeling here:_____
Now say to yourself...

1.
MY INTENTION IS TO REMIND MYSELF MANY TIMES TODAY...

FOCUSING ON THIS FEELING OF_____ IS MY REAL JOB FOR THE DAY.

2.
MY CURRENT CONDITIONS ARE IRRELEVANT BECAUSE...

I'M CREATING AN ENVIRONMENT THAT IS CAUSING THEM TO CHANGE.

3.
NO MORE SNAPSHOTS OF WHAT IS OR FEELING HELPLESS.

TODAY, I AM GOING TO USE THIS EMOTION AS MY BASE FEELING THAT WILL EFFECT FUTURE OUTCOMES.

Close your eyes again and reach for this intended feeing in
place of the feeling of current reality. Notice the softening
of your body as you aligning with source.

◀───▶

Write your chosen daily focused emotion reaching
for the feeling.

_____ _____ _____
_____ _____ _____
_____ _____ _____
_____ _____ _____

ASK YOURSELF MANY TIMES TODAY
"Is this the attracting vibration, I want the universe to respond to?"
If not, for the count of 10 long breaths in and
slowly letting them out.
Say and feel your chosen emotion in appreciation for the feeling.
It self-creates without any evidence needed.

• • • • • • • • • • • • • • • •

Write 3 things you would be interested in seeing that just for fun but
you are not worried about when.

_____
_____
_____

Let the universe show you these things in playful and exciting ways.

A THOUGHT REACHES A COMBUSTION POINT AT 16 SECONDS.

VIBRATIONAL CASH

A FULL 68 SECONDS ARE EQUIVALENT TO 2 MILLION MAN-HOURS.

Spend Your Vibrational Cash on one thing a day. If wanting a big ticket item slowly pay it off. This will make it more real for you.

The longer you spend feeling like the recipient of this desire the closer you are in being a match to it.

Focus on how it feels to buy this desire and the satisfaction attached within having it. Write about that satisfaction.

Close your eyes again and reach for the first thing that pops into your mind. No matter what the price tag is, big and small creations are all the same. Learn to start treating them all equal.

VibrationalCash

Date _____

Pay To The Order Of _____

5,000.00

IN YOUR CURRENCY

_____

LIVE THE EXPERIENCE IN THE NOW

FOR _____

SIGN NAME HERE

_____
_____
_____
_____
_____
_____
_____
_____
_____

ASK, BELIEVE,
RECEIVE

ASK

What are ready to take the vibrational journey to?
By asking for this desire it means you are creating a gap and your job is to close it.

BELIEVE/SOURCE

THE MINUTE YOU ASK, IT IS DONE VIBRATIONALLY COMPLETE AND 99.99% DONE PHYSICALLY

RECEIVE:

Create a momentum in belief by feeling it is yours for 20 second, snap shots at a time. Focusing only on feeling not image.

If you hold an emotion as the desire. You no longer are creating an impossibility. The shift from in the future having the desire becomes felt in the present moment, and you will notice the tension has left the solar plexus as you do this.
At this moment you are able to isolate the components of the desire even without having the desire. You become expectant, Being expectant is a very high frequency, and it is one step away from the manifestation to occur.

What do you feel ready to change in your life.
By asking you are now saying
"I will deliberately start creating this climate to close the gap.
I am aware of my part in how long the manifestation will take.

_____

_____

_____

_____

_____

Source has now become this vibrationally.
Your work is to create a mimicking or matching vibration.

Faith is created by reaching for the feeling and trusting the manifestation will follow.
Start now creating the feeling it is done by using small 20-second Virtual Realities while conjuring the emotions.
The idea is to preserve the focus that feels good longer, so you can match the frequency and enjoy the pleasures it provides in feelings.
Always leave the imagination play through, if you feel anything but enjoyment.

POSITIVE ASPECTS

Appreciation is one of the highest vibrations you can use to shift how you are feeling.
It will build momentum fast and create an overall positive experience.
Even when you are in the worst of moods, if you focus on the parts that
you are appreciative for you will begin to start a new point of attraction.

I APPRECIATE YOU!
PERSON
NAME: *WHY?*

_____
_____
_____
_____
_____

**I APPRECIATE THE
BEAUTY FOUND HERE.**
PLACE: *WHY?*

_____
_____
_____
_____

**I APPRECIATE THE
BEAUTY FOUND HERE.**
PLACE: *WHY?*

_____
_____
_____
_____

I APPRECIATE YOU!
PERSON
NAME: *WHY?*

_____
_____
_____
_____

**I APPRECIATE HAVING
ACCESS TO THIS.**
THING: *WHY?*

_____
_____
_____
_____

**WHAT I LOVE ABOUT
THE WEATHER:**   *WHY?*

_____
_____
_____
_____

I APPRECIATE YOU!
PERSON
NAME: *WHY?*

_____
_____
_____

**I APPRECIATE HAVING
ACCESS TO THIS.**
THING: *WHY?*

_____
_____
_____

WHAT I LOVE ABOUT..
WHY?

_____
_____
_____

POSITIVE
ASPECTS

Focus on anything and everything. Saying "thank you"
Creates more things to be thankful for.

I AM THANKFUL FOR: *WHY?*

_____
_____
_____
_____
_____

I AM THANKFUL FOR: *WHY?*

_____
_____
_____
_____
_____

I AM THANKFUL FOR: *WHY?*

_____
_____
_____
_____
_____

I AM THANKFUL FOR: *WHY?*

_____
_____
_____
_____
_____

I AM THANKFUL FOR: *WHY?*

_____
_____
_____
_____
_____

I AM THANKFUL FOR: *WHY?*

_____
_____
_____
_____
_____

I AM THANKFUL FOR: *WHY?*

_____
_____
_____
_____
_____

I AM THANKFUL FOR: *WHY?*

_____
_____
_____
_____
_____

I AM THANKFUL FOR: *WHY?*

_____
_____
_____
_____
_____

FOODS
yum! WHAT MY BODY ENJOYED TODAY

_____
_____
_____
_____
_____
_____

WATER INTAKE ✓
AM I HYDRATED?

GET PHYSICAL
WHAT MOVEMENT DID MY BODY ENJOY TODAY

_____
_____
_____
_____
_____

MEDITATION

SPEND 15 MINS FOCUSING ON REPETITIVE SOUND. THE MORE BORING IT IS THE BETTER.

A TO Z

WRITE WORDS FROM A TO Z FEELING FOR THEM AS YOU WRITE THEM MAKE UP WORDS IF YOU CANT THINK OF ONE.

A_____ B_____ C_____ D_____

E_____ F_____ G_____ H_____

I_____ J_____ K_____ L_____

M_____ N_____ O_____ P_____

Q_____ R_____ S_____ T_____

U_____ V_____ W_____ X_____

Y_____ Z_____

Am I match ____
If I am feeling ease and comfort in this moment then I am.
I will sit in the feeling of satisfaction at focusing on these emotions right now.

1 SIT FOR ONE MINUTE BREATHING

Focus on holding a smile while taking in long and deep breaths in and slowly letting them out. Relax your body and feel the comfort of where you sit.

2 REMIND YOURSELF HOW IMPORTANT IT IS TO FEEL GOOD.

Today, nothing is more important then I feel good.

3
Write that here:

_____

_____

_____

_____

_____

_____

5
NOTICE HOW THE SUN CAME UP AND THINGS ARE ALWAYS IN MOTION.

4
Close your eyes and see yourself aligning with source, blending into one.
Thank this constant focus upon you.

6
Feel and give thanks for the abundance of well-being all around.
For a full minute.

What 4 things would I like to turn over to the Universe to take care of for me today?

1._____

2._____

3._____

4._____

When you stop looking for the desired manifestation, you learn that the feeling grows and carries you to the destination.

Write what things you intend to do today and how you intend to feel as you accomplish these things.

1._____Feeling_____

2._____Feeling_____

3._____Feeling_____

4._____Feeling_____

I look forward to enjoying a productive and fun day.

Pick one of these emotions you would like to use
as today's intended feeling.
Ease, Relaxed, Comfort
Write this feeling here:_____
Now say to yourself...

1.
MY INTENTION IS TO REMIND MYSELF MANY TIMES TODAY...

FOCUSING ON THIS FEELING OF_____ IS MY REAL JOB FOR THE DAY.

2.
MY CURRENT CONDITIONS ARE IRRELEVANT BECAUSE...

I'M CREATING AN ENVIRONMENT THAT IS CAUSING THEM TO CHANGE.

3.
NO MORE SNAPSHOTS OF WHAT IS OR FEELING HELPLESS.

TODAY, I AM GOING TO USE THIS EMOTION AS MY BASE FEELING THAT WILL EFFECT FUTURE OUTCOMES.

Close your eyes again and reach for this intended feeing in place of the feeling of current reality. Notice the softening of your body as you aligning with source.

Write your chosen daily focused emotion reaching for the feeling.

_____ _____ _____
_____ _____ _____
_____ _____ _____
_____ _____ _____

ASK YOURSELF MANY TIMES TODAY
"Is this the attracting vibration, I want the universe to respond to?"
If not, for the count of 10 long breaths in and
slowly letting them out.
Say and feel your chosen emotion in appreciation for the feeling.
It self-creates without any evidence needed.

Write 3 things you would be interested in seeing that just for fun but you are not worried about when.

_____
_____
_____

Let the universe show you these things in playful and exciting ways.

A THOUGHT REACHES A COMBUSTION POINT AT 16 SECONDS.

VIBRATIONAL
CASH

A FULL 68 SECONDS ARE EQUIVALENT TO 2 MILLION MAN-HOURS.

Spend Your Vibrational Cash on one thing a day. If wanting a big ticket item slowly pay it off. This will make it more real for you.

The longer you spend feeling like the recipient of this desire the closer you are in being a match to it.

Focus on how it feels to buy this desire and the satisfaction attached within having it. Write about that satisfaction.

Close your eyes again and reach for the first thing that pops into your mind. No matter what the price tag is, big and small creations are all the same. Learn to start treating them all equal.

VIBRATIONAL CASH	DATE _____
PAY TO THE ORDER OF	**5,000.00**
	IN YOUR CURRENCY
_____	
LIVE THE EXPERIENCE IN THE NOW	
FOR _____	
	SIGN NAME HERE

_____

_____

_____

_____

_____

_____

_____

_____

_____

_____

ASK, BELIEVE,
RECEIVE

ASK

What are ready to take the vibrational journey to?
By asking for this desire it means you are creating a gap and your job is to close it.

BELIEVE/SOURCE

THE MINUTE YOU ASK, IT IS DONE VIBRATIONALLY COMPLETE AND 99.99% DONE PHYSICALLY

RECEIVE:

Create a momentum in belief by feeling it is yours for 20 second, snap shots at a time. Focusing only on feeling not image.

If you hold an emotion as the desire. You no longer are creating an impossibility. The shift from in the future having the desire becomes felt in the present moment, and you will notice the tension has left the solar plexus as you do this.
At this moment you are able to isolate the components of the desire even without having the desire. You become expectant, Being expectant is a very high frequency, and it is one step away from the manifestation to occur.

What do you feel ready to change in your life.
By asking you are now saying "I will deliberately start creating this climate to close the gap.
I am aware of my part in how long the manifestation will take.

_____
_____
_____
_____
_____

Source has now become this vibrationally.
Your work is to create a mimicking or matching vibration.

Faith is created by reaching for the feeling and trusting the manifestation will follow.
Start now creating the feeling it is done by using small 20-second Virtual Realities while conjuring the emotions.
The idea is to preserve the focus that feels good longer, so you can match the frequency and enjoy the pleasures it provides in feelings.
Always leave the imagination
play through, if you feel anything but enjoyment.

POSITIVE ASPECTS

Appreciation is one of the highest vibrations you can use to shift how you are feeling.
It will build momentum fast and create an overall positive experience.
Even when you are in the worst of moods, if you focus on the parts that
you are appreciative for you will begin to start a new point of attraction.

I APPRECIATE YOU!
PERSON NAME: *WHY?*

_____
_____
_____
_____
_____

I APPRECIATE THE BEAUTY FOUND HERE.
PLACE: *WHY?*

_____
_____
_____
_____
_____

I APPRECIATE THE BEAUTY FOUND HERE.
PLACE: *WHY?*

_____
_____
_____
_____
_____

I APPRECIATE YOU!
PERSON NAME: *WHY?*

_____
_____
_____
_____
_____

I APPRECIATE HAVING ACCESS TO THIS.
THING: *WHY?*

_____
_____
_____
_____
_____

WHAT I LOVE ABOUT THE WEATHER: *WHY?*

_____
_____
_____
_____
_____

I APPRECIATE YOU!
PERSON NAME: *WHY?*

_____
_____
_____
_____
_____

I APPRECIATE HAVING ACCESS TO THIS.
THING: *WHY?*

_____
_____
_____
_____
_____

WHAT I LOVE ABOUT..   *WHY?*

_____
_____
_____
_____
_____

POSITIVE
ASPECTS

Focus on anything and everything. Saying "thank you"
Creates more things to be thankful for.

I AM THANKFUL FOR: *WHY?*

_____
_____
_____
_____
_____

I AM THANKFUL FOR: *WHY?*

_____
_____
_____
_____
_____

I AM THANKFUL FOR: *WHY?*

_____
_____
_____
_____
_____

I AM THANKFUL FOR: *WHY?*

_____
_____
_____
_____
_____

I AM THANKFUL FOR: *WHY?*

_____
_____
_____
_____
_____

I AM THANKFUL FOR: *WHY?*

_____
_____
_____
_____
_____

I AM THANKFUL FOR: *WHY?*

_____
_____
_____
_____
_____

I AM THANKFUL FOR: *WHY?*

_____
_____
_____
_____
_____

I AM THANKFUL FOR: *WHY?*

_____
_____
_____
_____
_____

FOODS

yum! WHAT MY BODY ENJOYED TODAY

_____

_____

_____

_____

_____

_____

WATER INTAKE

AM I HYDRATED?

GET PHYSICAL

WHAT MOVEMENT DID MY BODY ENJOY TODAY

_____

_____

_____

_____

MEDITATION

SPEND 15 MINS FOCUSING ON REPETITIVE SOUND. THE MORE BORING IT IS THE BETTER.

A TO Z

WRITE WORDS FROM A TO Z FEELING FOR THEM AS YOU WRITE THEM MAKE UP WORDS IF YOU CANT THINK OF ONE.

A_____ B_____ C_____ D_____

E_____ F_____ G_____ H_____

I_____ J_____ K_____ L_____

M_____ N_____ O_____ P_____

Q_____ R_____ S_____ T_____

U_____ V_____ W_____ X_____

Y_____ Z_____

Am I match ____
If I am feeling ease and comfort in this moment then I am.
I will sit in the feeling of satisfaction at focusing on these emotions right now.

1 SIT FOR ONE MINUTE BREATHING

Focus on holding a smile while taking in long and deep breaths in and slowly letting them out. Relax your body and feel the comfort of where you sit.

2 REMIND YOURSELF HOW IMPORTANT IT IS TO FEEL GOOD.

Today, nothing is more important then I feel good.

3

Write that here:

_____
_____
_____
_____
_____
_____
_____

4

Close your eyes and see yourself aligning with source, blending into one.
Thank this constant focus upon you.

5

NOTICE HOW THE SUN CAME UP AND THINGS ARE ALWAYS IN MOTION.

6

Feel and give thanks for the abundance of well-being all around.
For a full minute.

What 4 things would I like to turn over to the Universe to take care of for me today?

1._____
2._____
3._____
4._____

When you stop looking for the desired manifestation, you learn that the feeling grows and carries you to the destination.

Write what things you intend to do today and how you intend to feel as you accomplish these things.

1._____Feeling_____
2._____Feeling_____
3._____Feeling_____
4._____Feeling_____

I look forward to enjoying a productive and fun day.

Pick one of these emotions you would like to use
as today's intended feeling.
Ease, Relaxed, Comfort
Write this feeling here:_____
Now say to yourself...

1.
MY INTENTION IS TO REMIND MYSELF MANY TIMES TODAY...

FOCUSING ON THIS FEELING OF_____
IS MY REAL JOB FOR THE DAY.

2.
MY CURRENT CONDITIONS ARE IRRELEVANT BECAUSE...

I'M CREATING AN ENVIRONMENT THAT IS CAUSING THEM TO CHANGE.

3.
NO MORE SNAPSHOTS OF WHAT IS OR FEELING HELPLESS.

TODAY, I AM GOING TO USE THIS EMOTION AS MY BASE FEELING THAT WILL EFFECT FUTURE OUTCOMES.

Close your eyes again and reach for this intended feeing in
place of the feeling of current reality. Notice the softening
of your body as you aligning with source.

Write your chosen daily focused emotion reaching
for the feeling.

_____ _____ _____
_____ _____ _____
_____ _____ _____
_____ _____ _____

ASK YOURSELF MANY TIMES TODAY
"Is this the attracting vibration, I want the universe to respond to?"
If not, for the count of 10 long breaths in and
slowly letting them out.
Say and feel your chosen emotion in appreciation for the feeling.
It self-creates without any evidence needed.

Write 3 things you would be interested in seeing that just for fun but
you are not worried about when.

_____
_____
_____

Let the universe show you these things in playful and exciting ways.

A THOUGHT REACHES A COMBUSTION POINT AT 16 SECONDS.

Spend Your Vibrational Cash on one thing a day. If wanting a big ticket item slowly pay it off. This will make it more real for you.

VIBRATIONAL CASH

The longer you spend feeling like the recipient of this desire the closer you are in being a match to it.

A FULL 68 SECONDS ARE EQUIVALENT TO 2 MILLION MAN-HOURS.

Focus on how it feels to buy this desire and the satisfaction attached within having it. Write about that satisfaction.

Close your eyes again and reach for the first thing that pops into your mind. No matter what the price tag is, big and small creations are all the same. Learn to start treating them all equal.

VIBRATIONAL CASH

DATE _____

PAY TO THE ORDER OF

5,000.00

IN YOUR CURRENCY

_____

LIVE THE EXPERIENCE IN THE NOW

FOR _____

SIGN NAME HERE

ASK, BELIEVE,
RECEIVE

ASK

What are ready to take the vibrational journey to?
By asking for this desire it means you are creating a gap and your job is to close it.

BELIEVE/SOURCE

THE MINUTE YOU ASK, IT IS DONE VIBRATIONALLY COMPLETE AND 99.99% DONE PHYSICALLY

RECEIVE:

Create a momentum in belief by feeling it is yours for 20 second, snap shots at a time. Focusing only on feeling not image.

If you hold an emotion as the desire. You no longer are creating an impossibility. The shift from in the future having the desire becomes felt in the present moment, and you will notice the tension has left the solar plexus as you do this.
At this moment you are able to isolate the components of the desire even without having the desire. You become expectant, Being expectant is a very high frequency, and it is one step away from the manifestation to occur.

What do you feel ready to change in your life.
By asking you are now saying "I will deliberately start creating this climate to close the gap.
I am aware of my part in how long the manifestation will take.

_____
_____
_____
_____
_____

Source has now become this vibrationally.
Your work is to create a mimicking or matching vibration.

Faith is created by reaching for the feeling and trusting the manifestation will follow.
Start now creating the feeling it is done by using small 20-second Virtual Realities while conjuring the emotions.
The idea is to preserve the focus that feels good longer, so you can match the frequency and enjoy the pleasures it provides in feelings.
Always leave the imagination play through, if you feel anything but enjoyment.

POSITIVE ASPECTS

Appreciation is one of the highest vibrations you can use to shift how you are feeling.
It will build momentum fast and create an overall positive experience.
Even when you are in the worst of moods, if you focus on the parts that
you are appreciative for you will begin to start a new point of attraction.

I APPRECIATE YOU!
PERSON
NAME: *WHY?*

_____
_____
_____
_____
_____

I APPRECIATE THE
BEAUTY FOUND HERE.
PLACE: *WHY?*

_____
_____
_____
_____
_____

I APPRECIATE THE
BEAUTY FOUND HERE.
PLACE: *WHY?*

_____
_____
_____
_____
_____

I APPRECIATE YOU!
PERSON
NAME: *WHY?*

_____
_____
_____
_____
_____

I APPRECIATE HAVING
ACCESS TO THIS.
THING: *WHY?*

_____
_____
_____
_____
_____

WHAT I LOVE ABOUT
THE WEATHER: *WHY?*

_____
_____
_____
_____
_____

I APPRECIATE YOU!
PERSON
NAME: *WHY?*

_____
_____
_____
_____

I APPRECIATE HAVING
ACCESS TO THIS.
THING: *WHY?*

_____
_____
_____
_____

WHAT I LOVE ABOUT..
                WHY?

_____
_____
_____
_____

POSITIVE
ASPECTS

Focus on anything and everything. Saying "thank you"
Creates more things to be thankful for.

I AM THANKFUL FOR: *WHY?*

_____
_____
_____
_____
_____

I AM THANKFUL FOR: *WHY?*

_____
_____
_____
_____
_____

I AM THANKFUL FOR: *WHY?*

_____
_____
_____
_____
_____

I AM THANKFUL FOR: *WHY?*

_____
_____
_____
_____
_____

I AM THANKFUL FOR: *WHY?*

_____
_____
_____
_____
_____

I AM THANKFUL FOR: *WHY?*

_____
_____
_____
_____
_____

I AM THANKFUL FOR: *WHY?*

_____
_____
_____
_____
_____

I AM THANKFUL FOR: *WHY?*

_____
_____
_____
_____
_____

I AM THANKFUL FOR: *WHY?*

_____
_____
_____
_____
_____

FOODS
yum! WHAT MY BODY ENJOYED TODAY

_____
_____
_____
_____
_____
_____

WATER INTAKE ✓
AM I HYDRATED?

GET PHYSICAL
WHAT MOVEMENT DID MY BODY ENJOY TODAY

_____
_____
_____
_____

MEDITATION

SPEND 15 MINS FOCUSING ON REPETITIVE SOUND. THE MORE BORING IT IS THE BETTER.

A TO Z

WRITE WORDS FROM A TO Z FEELING FOR THEM AS YOU WRITE THEM MAKE UP WORDS IF YOU CANT THINK OF ONE.

A_____ B_____ C_____ D_____

E_____ F_____ G_____ H_____

I_____ J_____ K_____ L_____

M_____ N_____ O_____ P_____

Q_____ R_____ S_____ T_____

U_____ V_____ W_____ X_____

Y_____ Z_____

Am I match ____
If I am feeling ease and comfort in this moment then I am.
I will sit in the feeling of satisfaction at focusing on these emotions right now.

1 **SIT FOR ONE MINUTE BREATHING**

Focus on holding a smile while taking in long and deep breaths in and slowly letting them out. Relax your body and feel the comfort of where you sit.

2 REMIND YOURSELF HOW IMPORTANT IT IS TO FEEL GOOD.

Today, nothing is more important then I feel good.

3
Write that here:

_____
_____
_____
_____
_____
_____

5 NOTICE HOW THE SUN CAME UP AND THINGS ARE ALWAYS IN MOTION.

4
Close your eyes and see yourself aligning with source, blending into one. Thank this constant focus upon you.

6
Feel and give thanks for the abundance of well-being all around. For a full minute.

What 4 things would I like to turn over to the Universe to take care of for me today?

1._____
2._____
3._____
4._____

When you stop looking for the desired manifestation, you learn that the feeling grows and carries you to the destination.

Write what things you intend to do today and how you intend to feel as you accomplish these things.

1._____Feeling_____
2._____Feeling_____
3._____Feeling_____
4._____Feeling_____

I look forward to enjoying a productive and fun day.

Pick one of these emotions you would like to use
as today's intended feeling.
Ease, Relaxed, Comfort
Write this feeling here:_____
Now say to yourself...

1.
MY INTENTION IS TO REMIND MYSELF MANY TIMES TODAY...

FOCUSING ON THIS FEELING OF_____ IS MY REAL JOB FOR THE DAY.

2.
MY CURRENT CONDITIONS ARE IRRELEVANT BECAUSE...

I'M CREATING AN ENVIRONMENT THAT IS CAUSING THEM TO CHANGE.

3.
NO MORE SNAPSHOTS OF WHAT IS OR FEELING HELPLESS.

TODAY, I AM GOING TO USE THIS EMOTION AS MY BASE FEELING THAT WILL EFFECT FUTURE OUTCOMES.

Close your eyes again and reach for this intended feeing in place of the feeling of current reality. Notice the softening of your body as you aligning with source.

Write your chosen daily focused emotion reaching for the feeling.

_____ _____ _____
_____ _____ _____
_____ _____ _____
_____ _____ _____

ASK YOURSELF MANY TIMES TODAY
"Is this the attracting vibration, I want the universe to respond to?"
If not, for the count of 10 long breaths in and
slowly letting them out.
Say and feel your chosen emotion in appreciation for the feeling.
It self-creates without any evidence needed.

Write 3 things you would be interested in seeing that just for fun but
you are not worried about when.

_____
_____
_____

Let the universe show you these things in playful and exciting ways.

A THOUGHT REACHES A COMBUSTION POINT AT 16 SECONDS.

VIBRATIONAL CASH

A FULL 68 SECONDS ARE EQUIVALENT TO 2 MILLION MAN-HOURS.

Spend Your Vibrational Cash on one thing a day. If wanting a big ticket item slowly pay it off. This will make it more real for you.

The longer you spend feeling like the recipient of this desire the closer you are in being a match to it.

Focus on how it feels to buy this desire and the satisfaction attached within having it. Write about that satisfaction.

Close your eyes again and reach for the first thing that pops into your mind. No matter what the price tag is, big and small creations are all the same. Learn to start treating them all equal.

VibrationalCash

Pay To The Order Of

Date

5,000.00

IN YOUR CURRENCY

LIVE THE EXPERIENCE IN THE NOW

FOR

Sign name here

_____
_____
_____
_____
_____
_____
_____
_____

ASK, BELIEVE,
RECEIVE

ASK

What are ready to take the vibrational journey to?
By asking for this desire it means you are creating a gap and your job is to close it.

BELIEVE/SOURCE

THE MINUTE YOU ASK, IT IS DONE VIBRATIONALLY COMPLETE AND 99.99% DONE PHYSICALLY

RECEIVE:

Create a momentum in belief by feeling it is yours for 20 second, snap shots at a time. Focusing only on feeling not image.

If you hold an emotion as the desire. You no longer are creating an impossibility. The shift from in the future having the desire becomes felt in the present moment, and you will notice the tension has left the solar plexus as you do this.
At this moment you are able to isolate the components of the desire even without having the desire. You become expectant, Being expectant is a very high frequency, and it is one step away from the manifestation to occur.

What do you feel ready to change in your life.
By asking you are now saying "I will deliberately start creating this climate to close the gap. I am aware of my part in how long the manifestation will take.

_____
_____
_____
_____
_____

Source has now become this vibrationally.
Your work is to create a mimicking or matching vibration.

Faith is created by reaching for the feeling and trusting the manifestation will follow.
Start now creating the feeling it is done by using small 20-second Virtual Realities while conjuring the emotions.
The idea is to preserve the focus that feels good longer, so you can match the frequency and enjoy the pleasures it provides in feelings.
Always leave the imagination play through, if you feel anything but enjoyment.

POSITIVE ASPECTS

Appreciation is one of the highest vibrations you can use to shift how you are feeling.
It will build momentum fast and create an overall positive experience.
Even when you are in the worst of moods, if you focus on the parts that
you are appreciative for you will begin to start a new point of attraction.

I APPRECIATE YOU!
PERSON
NAME: *WHY?*

_____
_____
_____
_____
_____

I APPRECIATE THE
BEAUTY FOUND HERE.
PLACE: *WHY?*

_____
_____
_____
_____
_____

I APPRECIATE THE
BEAUTY FOUND HERE.
PLACE: *WHY?*

_____
_____
_____
_____
_____

I APPRECIATE YOU!
PERSON
NAME: *WHY?*

_____
_____
_____
_____
_____

I APPRECIATE HAVING
ACCESS TO THIS.
THING: *WHY?*

_____
_____
_____
_____
_____

WHAT I LOVE ABOUT
THE WEATHER: *WHY?*

_____
_____
_____
_____
_____

I APPRECIATE YOU!
PERSON
NAME: *WHY?*

_____
_____
_____
_____
_____

I APPRECIATE HAVING
ACCESS TO THIS.
THING: *WHY?*

_____
_____
_____
_____
_____

WHAT I LOVE ABOUT..

               WHY?

_____
_____
_____
_____
_____

POSITIVE
ASPECTS

Focus on anything and everything. Saying "thank you"
Creates more things to be thankful for.

I AM THANKFUL FOR: *WHY?*

_____
_____
_____
_____
_____

I AM THANKFUL FOR: *WHY?*

_____
_____
_____
_____
_____

I AM THANKFUL FOR: *WHY?*

_____
_____
_____
_____
_____

I AM THANKFUL FOR: *WHY?*

_____
_____
_____
_____
_____

I AM THANKFUL FOR: *WHY?*

_____
_____
_____
_____
_____

I AM THANKFUL FOR: *WHY?*

_____
_____
_____
_____
_____

I AM THANKFUL FOR: *WHY?*

_____
_____
_____
_____

I AM THANKFUL FOR: *WHY?*

_____
_____
_____
_____

I AM THANKFUL FOR: *WHY?*

_____
_____
_____
_____

FOODS

yum! WHAT MY BODY ENJOYED TODAY

_____

_____

_____

_____

_____

_____

WATER INTAKE

AM I HYDRATED?

GET PHYSICAL

WHAT MOVEMENT DID MY BODY ENJOY TODAY

_____

_____

_____

_____

MEDITATION

SPEND 15 MINS FOCUSING ON REPETITIVE SOUND. THE MORE BORING IT IS THE BETTER.

A TO Z

WRITE WORDS FROM A TO Z FEELING FOR THEM AS YOU WRITE THEM MAKE UP WORDS IF YOU CANT THINK OF ONE.

A_____ B_____ C_____ D_____

E_____ F_____ G_____ H_____

I_____ J_____ K_____ L_____

M_____ N_____ O_____ P_____

Q_____ R_____ S_____ T_____

U_____ V_____ W_____ X_____

Y_____ Z_____

Am I match ____
If I am feeling ease and comfort in this moment then I am.
I will sit in the feeling of satisfaction at focusing on these emotions right now.

1 SIT FOR ONE MINUTE BREATHING

Focus on holding a smile while taking in long and deep breaths in and slowly letting them out. Relax your body and feel the comfort of where you sit.

2 REMIND YOURSELF HOW IMPORTANT IT IS TO FEEL GOOD.

Today, nothing is more important then I feel good.

3

Write that here:

_____

_____

_____

_____

_____

_____

_____

5

NOTICE HOW THE SUN CAME UP AND THINGS ARE ALWAYS IN MOTION.

4

Close your eyes and see yourself aligning with source, blending into one. Thank this constant focus upon you.

6

Feel and give thanks for the abundance of well-being all around. For a full minute.

What 4 things would I like to turn over to the Universe to take care of for me today?

⬅⟶

1._____

2._____

3._____

4._____

When you stop looking for the desired manifestation, you learn that the feeling grows and carries you to the destination.

Write what things you intend to do today and how you intend to feel as you accomplish these things.

1._____Feeling_____

2._____Feeling_____

3._____Feeling_____

4._____Feeling_____

I look forward to enjoying a productive and fun day.

Pick one of these emotions you would like to use
as today's intended feeling.
Ease, Relaxed, Comfort
Write this feeling here:_____
Now say to yourself...

1.
MY INTENTION IS TO REMIND MYSELF MANY TIMES TODAY...

FOCUSING ON THIS FEELING OF_____ IS MY REAL JOB FOR THE DAY.

2.
MY CURRENT CONDITIONS ARE IRRELEVANT BECAUSE...

I'M CREATING AN ENVIRONMENT THAT IS CAUSING THEM TO CHANGE.

3.
NO MORE SNAPSHOTS OF WHAT IS OR FEELING HELPLESS.

TODAY, I AM GOING TO USE THIS EMOTION AS MY BASE FEELING THAT WILL EFFECT FUTURE OUTCOMES.

Close your eyes again and reach for this intended feeing in place of the feeling of current reality. Notice the softening of your body as you aligning with source.

⬅ ➡

Write your chosen daily focused emotion reaching for the feeling.

_____ _____ _____
_____ _____ _____
_____ _____ _____
_____ _____ _____

ASK YOURSELF MANY TIMES TODAY
"Is this the attracting vibration, I want the universe to respond to?"
If not, for the count of 10 long breaths in and
slowly letting them out.
Say and feel your chosen emotion in appreciation for the feeling.
It self-creates without any evidence needed.

Write 3 things you would be interested in seeing that just for fun but you are not worried about when.

_____
_____
_____

Let the universe show you these things in playful and exciting ways.

A THOUGHT REACHES A COMBUSTION POINT AT 16 SECONDS.

Spend Your Vibrational Cash on one thing a day. If wanting a big ticket item slowly pay it off. This will make it more real for you.

VIBRATIONAL CASH

The longer you spend feeling like the recipient of this desire the closer you are in being a match to it.

A FULL 68 SECONDS ARE EQUIVALENT TO 2 MILLION MAN-HOURS.

Focus on how it feels to buy this desire and the satisfaction attached within having it. Write about that satisfaction.

Close your eyes again and reach for the first thing that pops into your mind. No matter what the price tag is, big and small creations are all the same. Learn to start treating them all equal.

VIBRATIONAL CASH

DATE _____

PAY TO THE ORDER OF _____

5,000.00

IN YOUR CURRENCY

_____

LIVE THE EXPERIENCE IN THE NOW

FOR _____   SIGN NAME HERE _____

_____
_____
_____
_____
_____
_____
_____
_____

ASK, BELIEVE,
RECEIVE

ASK

What are ready to take the vibrational journey to?
By asking for this desire it means you are creating a gap and your job is to close it.

BELIEVE/SOURCE

THE MINUTE YOU ASK, IT IS DONE VIBRATIONALLY COMPLETE AND 99.99% DONE PHYSICALLY

RECEIVE:

Create a momentum in belief by feeling it is yours for 20 second, snap shots at a time. Focusing only on feeling not image.

If you hold an emotion as the desire. You no longer are creating an impossibility. The shift from in the future having the desire becomes felt in the present moment, and you will notice the tension has left the solar plexus as you do this.
At this moment you are able to isolate the components of the desire even without having the desire. You become expectant, Being expectant is a very high frequency, and it is one step away from the manifestation to occur.

What do you feel ready to change in your life.
By asking you are now saying "I will deliberately start creating this climate to close the gap.
I am aware of my part in how long the manifestation will take.

_____
_____
_____
_____
_____

Source has now become this vibrationally.
Your work is to create a mimicking or matching vibration.

Faith is created by reaching for the feeling and trusting the manifestation will follow.
Start now creating the feeling it is done by using small 20-second Virtual Realities while conjuring the emotions.
The idea is to preserve the focus that feels good longer, so you can match the frequency and enjoy the pleasures it provides in feelings.
Always leave the imagination
play through, if you feel anything but enjoyment.

POSITIVE ASPECTS

Appreciation is one of the highest vibrations you can use to shift how you are feeling.
It will build momentum fast and create an overall positive experience.
Even when you are in the worst of moods, if you focus on the parts that
you are appreciative for you will begin to start a new point of attraction.

I APPRECIATE YOU!
PERSON
NAME: *WHY?*

_____
_____
_____
_____
_____

I APPRECIATE THE
BEAUTY FOUND HERE.
PLACE: *WHY?*

_____
_____
_____
_____

I APPRECIATE THE
BEAUTY FOUND HERE.
PLACE: *WHY?*

_____
_____
_____
_____

I APPRECIATE YOU!
PERSON
NAME: *WHY?*

_____
_____
_____
_____
_____

I APPRECIATE HAVING
ACCESS TO THIS.
THING: *WHY?*

_____
_____
_____
_____

WHAT I LOVE ABOUT
THE WEATHER: *WHY?*

_____
_____
_____
_____

I APPRECIATE YOU!
PERSON
NAME: *WHY?*

_____
_____
_____
_____

I APPRECIATE HAVING
ACCESS TO THIS.
THING: *WHY?*

_____
_____
_____
_____

WHAT I LOVE ABOUT..

WHY?

_____
_____
_____
_____

POSITIVE
ASPECTS

Focus on anything and everything. Saying "thank you"
Creates more things to be thankful for.

I AM THANKFUL FOR: *WHY?*

_____
_____
_____
_____
_____

I AM THANKFUL FOR: *WHY?*

_____
_____
_____
_____
_____

I AM THANKFUL FOR: *WHY?*

_____
_____
_____
_____
_____

I AM THANKFUL FOR: *WHY?*

_____
_____
_____
_____
_____

I AM THANKFUL FOR: *WHY?*

_____
_____
_____
_____
_____

I AM THANKFUL FOR: *WHY?*

_____
_____
_____
_____
_____

I AM THANKFUL FOR: *WHY?*

_____
_____
_____
_____
_____

I AM THANKFUL FOR: *WHY?*

_____
_____
_____
_____
_____

I AM THANKFUL FOR: *WHY?*

_____
_____
_____
_____
_____

FOODS

yum! WHAT MY BODY ENJOYED TODAY

_____
_____
_____
_____
_____
_____

WATER INTAKE ✓

AM I HYDRATED?

GET PHYSICAL

WHAT MOVEMENT DID MY BODY ENJOY TODAY

_____
_____
_____
_____
_____

MEDITATION

SPEND 15 MINS FOCUSING ON REPETITIVE SOUND. THE MORE BORING IT IS THE BETTER.

A TO Z

WRITE WORDS FROM A TO Z FEELING FOR THEM AS YOU WRITE THEM MAKE UP WORDS IF YOU CANT THINK OF ONE.

A_____ B_____ C_____ D_____

E_____ F_____ G_____ H_____

I_____ J_____ K_____ L_____

M_____ N_____ O_____ P_____

Q_____ R_____ S_____ T_____

U_____ V_____ W_____ X_____

Y_____ Z_____

Am I match ____
If I am feeling ease and comfort in this moment then I am.
I will sit in the feeling of satisfaction at focusing on these emotions right now.

1 SIT FOR ONE MINUTE BREATHING

Focus on holding a smile while taking in long and deep breaths in and slowly letting them out. Relax your body and feel the comfort of where you sit.

2 REMIND YOURSELF HOW IMPORTANT IT IS TO FEEL GOOD.

Today, nothing is more important then I feel good.

3
Write that here:

_____
_____
_____
_____
_____
_____

5 NOTICE HOW THE SUN CAME UP AND THINGS ARE ALWAYS IN MOTION.

4
Close your eyes and see yourself aligning with source, blending into one.
Thank this constant focus upon you.

6
Feel and give thanks for the abundance of well-being all around.
For a full minute.

What 4 things would I like to turn over to the Universe to take care of for me today?

1._____
2._____
3._____
4._____

When you stop looking for the desired manifestation, you learn that the feeling grows and carries you to the destination.

Write what things you intend to do today and how you intend to feel as you accomplish these things.

1._____Feeling_____
2._____Feeling_____
3._____Feeling_____
4._____Feeling_____

I look forward to enjoying a productive and fun day.

Pick one of these emotions you would like to use
as today's intended feeling.
Ease, Relaxed, Comfort
Write this feeling here:_____
Now say to yourself...

1.
MY INTENTION IS TO REMIND MYSELF MANY TIMES TODAY...

FOCUSING ON THIS FEELING OF_____ IS MY REAL JOB FOR THE DAY.

2.
MY CURRENT CONDITIONS ARE IRRELEVANT BECAUSE...

I'M CREATING AN ENVIRONMENT THAT IS CAUSING THEM TO CHANGE.

3.
NO MORE SNAPSHOTS OF WHAT IS OR FEELING HELPLESS.

TODAY, I AM GOING TO USE THIS EMOTION AS MY BASE FEELING THAT WILL EFFECT FUTURE OUTCOMES.

Close your eyes again and reach for this intended feeing in place of the feeling of current reality. Notice the softening of your body as you aligning with source.

Write your chosen daily focused emotion reaching for the feeling.

_____ _____ _____
_____ _____ _____
_____ _____ _____
_____ _____ _____

ASK YOURSELF MANY TIMES TODAY
"Is this the attracting vibration, I want the universe to respond to?"
If not, for the count of 10 long breaths in and
slowly letting them out.
Say and feel your chosen emotion in appreciation for the feeling.
It self-creates without any evidence needed.

Write 3 things you would be interested in seeing that just for fun but you are not worried about when.

_____
_____
_____

Let the universe show you these things in playful and exciting ways.

A THOUGHT REACHES A COMBUSTION POINT AT 16 SECONDS.

VIBRATIONAL CASH

A FULL 68 SECONDS ARE EQUIVALENT TO 2 MILLION MAN-HOURS.

Spend Your Vibrational Cash on one thing a day. If wanting a big ticket item slowly pay it off. This will make it more real for you.

The longer you spend feeling like the recipient of this desire the closer you are in being a match to it.

Focus on how it feels to buy this desire and the satisfaction attached within having it. Write about that satisfaction.

Close your eyes again and reach for the first thing that pops into your mind. No matter what the price tag is, big and small creations are all the same. Learn to start treating them all equal.

VibrationalCash

Pay To The Order Of

Date

5,000.00

IN YOUR CURRENCY

LIVE THE EXPERIENCE IN THE NOW

FOR

Sign Name Here

ASK, BELIEVE,
RECEIVE

ASK

What are ready to take the vibrational journey to?
By asking for this desire it means you are creating a gap and your job is to close it.

BELIEVE/SOURCE

THE MINUTE YOU ASK, IT IS DONE VIBRATIONALLY COMPLETE AND 99.99% DONE PHYSICALLY

RECEIVE:

Create a momentum in belief by feeling it is yours for 20 second, snap shots at a time. Focusing only on feeling not image.

If you hold an emotion as the desire. You no longer are creating an impossibility. The shift from in the future having the desire becomes felt in the present moment, and you will notice the tension has left the solar plexus as you do this.
At this moment you are able to isolate the components of the desire even without having the desire. You become expectant, Being expectant is a very high frequency, and it is one step away from the manifestation to occur.

What do you feel ready to change in your life.
By asking you are now saying "I will deliberately start creating this climate to close the gap.
I am aware of my part in how long the manifestation will take.

_____
_____
_____
_____
_____

Source has now become this vibrationally.
Your work is to create a mimicking or matching vibration.

Faith is created by reaching for the feeling and trusting the manifestation will follow.
Start now creating the feeling it is done by using small 20-second Virtual Realities while conjuring the emotions.
The idea is to preserve the focus that feels good longer, so you can match the frequency and enjoy the pleasures it provides in feelings.
Always leave the imagination play through, if you feel anything but enjoyment.

POSITIVE ASPECTS

Appreciation is one of the highest vibrations you can use to shift how you are feeling.
It will build momentum fast and create an overall positive experience.
Even when you are in the worst of moods, if you focus on the parts that
you are appreciative for you will begin to start a new point of attraction.

I APPRECIATE YOU! PERSON NAME: *WHY?*

_____
_____
_____
_____
_____

I APPRECIATE THE BEAUTY FOUND HERE. PLACE: *WHY?*

_____
_____
_____
_____
_____

I APPRECIATE THE BEAUTY FOUND HERE. PLACE: *WHY?*

_____
_____
_____
_____
_____

I APPRECIATE YOU! PERSON NAME: *WHY?*

_____
_____
_____
_____
_____

I APPRECIATE HAVING ACCESS TO THIS. THING: *WHY?*

_____
_____
_____
_____
_____

WHAT I LOVE ABOUT THE WEATHER: *WHY?*

_____
_____
_____
_____
_____

I APPRECIATE YOU! PERSON NAME: *WHY?*

_____
_____
_____
_____
_____

I APPRECIATE HAVING ACCESS TO THIS. THING: *WHY?*

_____
_____
_____
_____
_____

WHAT I LOVE ABOUT.. *WHY?*

_____
_____
_____
_____
_____

POSITIVE
ASPECTS

Focus on anything and everything. Saying "thank you"
Creates more things to be thankful for.

I AM THANKFUL FOR: *WHY?*

_____
_____
_____
_____
_____

I AM THANKFUL FOR: *WHY?*

_____
_____
_____
_____
_____

I AM THANKFUL FOR: *WHY?*

_____
_____
_____
_____
_____

I AM THANKFUL FOR: *WHY?*

_____
_____
_____
_____
_____

I AM THANKFUL FOR: *WHY?*

_____
_____
_____
_____
_____

I AM THANKFUL FOR: *WHY?*

_____
_____
_____
_____
_____

I AM THANKFUL FOR: *WHY?*

_____
_____
_____
_____
_____

I AM THANKFUL FOR: *WHY?*

_____
_____
_____
_____
_____

I AM THANKFUL FOR: *WHY?*

_____
_____
_____
_____
_____

FOODS
yum! **WHAT MY BODY ENJOYED TODAY**

_____
_____
_____
_____
_____
_____

WATER INTAKE
AM I HYDRATED? ✓

GET PHYSICAL
WHAT MOVEMENT DID MY BODY ENJOY TODAY

_____
_____
_____
_____
_____

MEDITATION

SPEND 15 MINS FOCUSING ON REPETITIVE SOUND. THE MORE BORING IT IS THE BETTER.

A TO Z

WRITE WORDS FROM A TO Z FEELING FOR THEM AS YOU WRITE THEM MAKE UP WORDS IF YOU CANT THINK OF ONE.

A_____ B_____ C_____ D_____

E_____ F_____ G_____ H_____

I_____ J_____ K_____ L_____

M_____ N_____ O_____ P_____

Q_____ R_____ S_____ T_____

U_____ V_____ W_____ X_____

Y_____ Z_____

Am I match ____
If I am feeling ease and comfort in this moment then I am.
I will sit in the feeling of satisfaction at focusing on these emotions right now.

1 SIT FOR ONE MINUTE BREATHING

Focus on holding a smile while taking in long and deep breaths in and slowly letting them out. Relax your body and feel the comfort of where you sit.

2 REMIND YOURSELF HOW IMPORTANT IT IS TO FEEL GOOD.

Today, nothing is more important then I feel good.

3

Write that here:

_____
_____
_____
_____
_____
_____

5

NOTICE HOW THE SUN CAME UP AND THINGS ARE ALWAYS IN MOTION.

4

Close your eyes and see yourself aligning with source, blending into one.
Thank this constant focus upon you.

6

Feel and give thanks for the abundance of well-being all around.
For a full minute.

What 4 things would I like to turn over to the Universe to take care of for me today?

1._____
2._____
3._____
4._____

When you stop looking for the desired manifestation,
you learn that the feeling grows and carries you to the destination.

Write what things you intend to do today
and how you intend to feel as you accomplish these things.

1._____Feeling_____
2._____Feeling_____
3._____Feeling_____
4._____Feeling_____

I look forward to enjoying a productive and fun day.

Pick one of these emotions you would like to use
as today's intended feeling.
Ease, Relaxed, Comfort
Write this feeling here:_____
Now say to yourself...

1.
MY INTENTION IS TO REMIND MYSELF MANY TIMES TODAY...

FOCUSING ON THIS FEELING OF_____ IS MY REAL JOB FOR THE DAY.

2.
MY CURRENT CONDITIONS ARE IRRELEVANT BECAUSE...

I'M CREATING AN ENVIRONMENT THAT IS CAUSING THEM TO CHANGE.

3.
NO MORE SNAPSHOTS OF WHAT IS OR FEELING HELPLESS.

TODAY, I AM GOING TO USE THIS EMOTION AS MY BASE FEELING THAT WILL EFFECT FUTURE OUTCOMES.

Close your eyes again and reach for this intended feeing in place of the feeling of current reality. Notice the softening of your body as you aligning with source.

Write your chosen daily focused emotion reaching for the feeling.

_____ _____ _____
_____ _____ _____
_____ _____ _____
_____ _____ _____

ASK YOURSELF MANY TIMES TODAY
"Is this the attracting vibration, I want the universe to respond to?"
If not, for the count of 10 long breaths in and
slowly letting them out.
Say and feel your chosen emotion in appreciation for the feeling.
It self-creates without any evidence needed.

Write 3 things you would be interested in seeing that just for fun but you are not worried about when.

_____
_____
_____

Let the universe show you these things in playful and exciting ways.

A THOUGHT REACHES A COMBUSTION POINT AT 16 SECONDS.

VIBRATIONAL CASH

A FULL 68 SECONDS ARE EQUIVALENT TO 2 MILLION MAN-HOURS.

Spend Your Vibrational Cash on one thing a day. If wanting a big ticket item slowly pay it off. This will make it more real for you.

The longer you spend feeling like the recipient of this desire the closer you are in being a match to it.

Focus on how it feels to buy this desire and the satisfaction attached within having it. Write about that satisfaction.

Close your eyes again and reach for the first thing that pops into your mind. No matter what the price tag is, big and small creations are all the same. Learn to start treating them all equal.

VIBRATIONAL CASH

DATE _____

PAY TO THE ORDER OF

_5,000.00_

IN YOUR CURRENCY

_____

LIVE THE EXPERIENCE IN THE NOW

FOR _____

SIGN NAME HERE

_____
_____
_____
_____
_____
_____
_____
_____
_____

ASK, BELIEVE,
RECEIVE

ASK

What are ready to take the vibrational journey to?
By asking for this desire it means you are creating a gap and your job is to close it.

BELIEVE/SOURCE

THE MINUTE YOU ASK, IT IS DONE VIBRATIONALLY COMPLETE AND 99.99% DONE PHYSICALLY

RECEIVE:

Create a momentum in belief by feeling it is yours for 20 second, snap shots at a time. Focusing only on feeling not image.

If you hold an emotion as the desire. You no longer are creating an impossibility. The shift from in the future having the desire becomes felt in the present moment, and you will notice the tension has left the solar plexus as you do this.
At this moment you are able to isolate the components of the desire even without having the desire. You become expectant, Being expectant is a very high frequency, and it is one step away from the manifestation to occur.

What do you feel ready to change in your life.
By asking you are now saying "I will deliberately start creating this climate to close the gap.
I am aware of my part in how long the manifestation will take.

_____
_____
_____
_____
_____

Source has now become this vibrationally.
Your work is to create a mimicking or matching vibration.

Faith is created by reaching for the feeling and trusting the manifestation will follow.
Start now creating the feeling it is done by using small 20-second Virtual Realities while conjuring the emotions.
The idea is to preserve the focus that feels good longer, so you can match the frequency and enjoy the pleasures it provides in feelings.
Always leave the imagination play through, if you feel anything but enjoyment.

POSITIVE ASPECTS

Appreciation is one of the highest vibrations you can use to shift how you are feeling.
It will build momentum fast and create an overall positive experience.
Even when you are in the worst of moods, if you focus on the parts that
you are appreciative for you will begin to start a new point of attraction.

I APPRECIATE YOU!
PERSON
NAME: *WHY?*

_____
_____
_____
_____
_____

I APPRECIATE THE BEAUTY FOUND HERE.
PLACE: *WHY?*

_____
_____
_____
_____

I APPRECIATE THE BEAUTY FOUND HERE.
PLACE: *WHY?*

_____
_____
_____
_____

I APPRECIATE YOU!
PERSON
NAME: *WHY?*

_____
_____
_____
_____

I APPRECIATE HAVING ACCESS TO THIS.
THING: *WHY?*

_____
_____
_____
_____

WHAT I LOVE ABOUT THE WEATHER: *WHY?*

_____
_____
_____
_____

I APPRECIATE YOU!
PERSON
NAME: *WHY?*

_____
_____
_____
_____

I APPRECIATE HAVING ACCESS TO THIS.
THING: *WHY?*

_____
_____
_____
_____

WHAT I LOVE ABOUT.. *WHY?*

_____
_____
_____
_____

POSITIVE
ASPECTS

Focus on anything and everything. Saying "thank you"
Creates more things to be thankful for.

I AM THANKFUL
FOR: *WHY?*

_____
_____
_____
_____
_____

I AM THANKFUL
FOR: *WHY?*

_____
_____
_____
_____
_____

I AM THANKFUL
FOR: *WHY?*

_____
_____
_____
_____
_____

I AM THANKFUL
FOR: *WHY?*

_____
_____
_____
_____
_____

I AM THANKFUL
FOR: *WHY?*

_____
_____
_____
_____
_____

I AM THANKFUL
FOR: *WHY?*

_____
_____
_____
_____
_____

I AM THANKFUL
FOR: *WHY?*

_____
_____
_____
_____
_____

I AM THANKFUL
FOR: *WHY?*

_____
_____
_____
_____
_____

I AM THANKFUL
FOR: *WHY?*

_____
_____
_____
_____
_____

FOODS

yum! WHAT MY BODY
ENJOYED TODAY

_____
_____
_____
_____
_____
_____

WATER INTAKE ✓

AM I
HYDRATED?

GET PHYSICAL

WHAT
MOVEMENT DID MY
BODY ENJOY TODAY

_____
_____
_____
_____
_____

MEDITATION

SPEND 15 MINS FOCUSING
ON REPETITIVE SOUND.
THE MORE BORING IT IS THE
BETTER.

A TO Z

WRITE WORDS FROM A TO Z
FEELING FOR THEM AS YOU
WRITE THEM MAKE UP
WORDS IF YOU CANT THINK
OF ONE.

A_____ B_____ C_____ D_____

E_____ F_____ G_____ H_____

I_____ J_____ K_____ L_____

M_____ N_____ O_____ P_____

Q_____ R_____ S_____ T_____

U_____ V_____ W_____ X_____

Y_____ Z_____

Am I match ____
If I am feeling ease and comfort in this moment then I am.
I will sit in the feeling of satisfaction at focusing on these emotions right
now.

1 SIT FOR ONE MINUTE BREATHING

Focus on holding a smile while taking in long and deep breaths in and slowly letting them out. Relax your body and feel the comfort of where you sit.

2 REMIND YOURSELF HOW IMPORTANT IT IS TO FEEL GOOD.

Today, nothing is more important then I feel good.

3

Write that here:

_____
_____
_____
_____
_____
_____
_____

5 NOTICE HOW THE SUN CAME UP AND THINGS ARE ALWAYS IN MOTION.

4

Close your eyes and see yourself aligning with source, blending into one. Thank this constant focus upon you.

6

Feel and give thanks for the abundance of well-being all around. For a full minute.

What 4 things would I like to turn over to the Universe to take care of for me today?

1._____
2._____
3._____
4._____

When you stop looking for the desired manifestation, you learn that the feeling grows and carries you to the destination.

Write what things you intend to do today and how you intend to feel as you accomplish these things.

1._____Feeling_____
2._____Feeling_____
3._____Feeling_____
4._____Feeling_____

I look forward to enjoying a productive and fun day.

Pick one of these emotions you would like to use
as today's intended feeling.
Ease, Relaxed, Comfort
Write this feeling here:_____
Now say to yourself...

1.
**MY INTENTION IS TO
REMIND MYSELF
MANY TIMES
TODAY...**

FOCUSING ON THIS
FEELING OF_____
IS MY REAL
JOB FOR THE DAY.

2.
**MY CURRENT
CONDITIONS ARE
IRRELEVANT
BECAUSE...**

I'M CREATING AN
ENVIRONMENT THAT
IS CAUSING THEM TO
CHANGE.

3.
**NO MORE SNAPSHOTS
OF WHAT IS
OR FEELING HELPLESS.**

TODAY, I AM GOING
TO USE THIS EMOTION
AS MY BASE FEELING
THAT WILL EFFECT
FUTURE OUTCOMES.

Close your eyes again and reach for this intended feeing in
place of the feeling of current reality. Notice the softening
of your body as you aligning with source.

Write your chosen daily focused emotion reaching
for the feeling.

_____ _____ _____
_____ _____ _____
_____ _____ _____
_____ _____ _____

ASK YOURSELF MANY TIMES TODAY
"Is this the attracting vibration, I want the universe to respond to?"
If not, for the count of 10 long breaths in and
slowly letting them out.
Say and feel your chosen emotion in appreciation for the feeling.
It self-creates without any evidence needed.

Write 3 things you would be interested in seeing that just for fun but
you are not worried about when.

_____
_____
_____

Let the universe show you these things in playful and exciting ways.

A THOUGHT REACHES A COMBUSTION POINT AT 16 SECONDS.

Spend Your Vibrational Cash on one thing a day. If wanting a big ticket item slowly pay it off. This will make it more real for you.

VIBRATIONAL
CASH

The longer you spend feeling like the recipient of this desire the closer you are in being a match to it.

A FULL 68 SECONDS ARE EQUIVALENT TO 2 MILLION MAN-HOURS.

Focus on how it feels to buy this desire and the satisfaction attached within having it. Write about that satisfaction.

Close your eyes again and reach for the first thing that pops into your mind. No matter what the price tag is, big and small creations are all the same. Learn to start treating them all equal.

VIBRATIONALCASH

DATE _____

PAY TO
THE ORDER OF _____

5,000.00

IN YOUR CURRENCY

LIVE THE EXPERIENCE IN THE NOW

FOR _____

SIGN NAME HERE

_____
_____
_____
_____
_____
_____
_____
_____
_____

ASK, BELIEVE,
RECEIVE

ASK

What are ready to take the vibrational journey to?
By asking for this desire it means you are creating a gap and your job is to close it.

BELIEVE/SOURCE

THE MINUTE YOU ASK, IT IS DONE VIBRATIONALLY COMPLETE AND 99.99% DONE PHYSICALLY

RECEIVE:

Create a momentum in belief by feeling it is yours for 20 second, snap shots at a time. Focusing only on feeling not image.

If you hold an emotion as the desire. You no longer are creating an impossibility. The shift from in the future having the desire becomes felt in the present moment, and you will notice the tension has left the solar plexus as you do this.
At this moment you are able to isolate the components of the desire even without having the desire. You become expectant, Being expectant is a very high frequency, and it is one step away from the manifestation to occur.

← →

What do you feel ready to change in your life.
By asking you are now saying "I will deliberately start creating this climate to close the gap.
I am aware of my part in how long the manifestation will take.

_____
_____
_____
_____
_____

Source has now become this vibrationally.
Your work is to create a mimicking or matching vibration.

Faith is created by reaching for the feeling and trusting the manifestation will follow.
Start now creating the feeling it is done by using small 20-second Virtual Realities while conjuring the emotions.
The idea is to preserve the focus that feels good longer, so you can match the frequency and enjoy the pleasures it provides in feelings.
Always leave the imagination
play through, if you feel anything but enjoyment.

POSITIVE ASPECTS

Appreciation is one of the highest vibrations you can use to shift how you are feeling.
It will build momentum fast and create an overall positive experience.
Even when you are in the worst of moods, if you focus on the parts that
you are appreciative for you will begin to start a new point of attraction.

I APPRECIATE YOU!
PERSON
NAME: *WHY?*

_____
_____
_____
_____
_____

I APPRECIATE THE
BEAUTY FOUND HERE.
PLACE: *WHY?*

_____
_____
_____
_____
_____

I APPRECIATE THE
BEAUTY FOUND HERE.
PLACE: *WHY?*

_____
_____
_____
_____
_____

I APPRECIATE YOU!
PERSON
NAME: *WHY?*

_____
_____
_____
_____
_____

I APPRECIATE HAVING
ACCESS TO THIS.
THING: *WHY?*

_____
_____
_____
_____
_____

WHAT I LOVE ABOUT
THE WEATHER: *WHY?*

_____
_____
_____
_____
_____

I APPRECIATE YOU!
PERSON
NAME: *WHY?*

_____
_____
_____
_____

I APPRECIATE HAVING
ACCESS TO THIS.
THING: *WHY?*

_____
_____
_____
_____

WHAT I LOVE ABOUT..
                 WHY?

_____
_____
_____
_____

POSITIVE
ASPECTS

Focus on anything and everything. Saying "thank you"
Creates more things to be thankful for.

I AM THANKFUL FOR: *WHY?*

_____
_____
_____
_____
_____

I AM THANKFUL FOR: *WHY?*

_____
_____
_____
_____
_____

I AM THANKFUL FOR: *WHY?*

_____
_____
_____
_____
_____

I AM THANKFUL FOR: *WHY?*

_____
_____
_____
_____
_____

I AM THANKFUL FOR: *WHY?*

_____
_____
_____
_____
_____

I AM THANKFUL FOR: *WHY?*

_____
_____
_____
_____
_____

I AM THANKFUL FOR: *WHY?*

_____
_____
_____
_____
_____

I AM THANKFUL FOR: *WHY?*

_____
_____
_____
_____
_____

I AM THANKFUL FOR: *WHY?*

_____
_____
_____
_____
_____

FOODS

yum! WHAT MY BODY ENJOYED TODAY

_____

_____

_____

_____

_____

_____

WATER INTAKE

AM I HYDRATED? ✓

GET PHYSICAL

WHAT MOVEMENT DID MY BODY ENJOY TODAY

_____

_____

_____

_____

MEDITATION

SPEND 15 MINS FOCUSING ON REPETITIVE SOUND. THE MORE BORING IT IS THE BETTER.

A TO Z

WRITE WORDS FROM A TO Z FEELING FOR THEM AS YOU WRITE THEM MAKE UP WORDS IF YOU CANT THINK OF ONE.

A_____ B_____ C_____ D_____

E_____ F_____ G_____ H_____

I_____ J_____ K_____ L_____

M_____ N_____ O_____ P_____

Q_____ R_____ S_____ T_____

U_____ V_____ W_____ X_____

Y_____ Z_____

Am I match ____
If I am feeling ease and comfort in this moment then I am.
I will sit in the feeling of satisfaction at focusing on these emotions right now.

1 SIT FOR ONE MINUTE BREATHING

Focus on holding a smile while taking in long and deep breaths in and slowly letting them out. Relax your body and feel the comfort of where you sit.

2 REMIND YOURSELF HOW IMPORTANT IT IS TO FEEL GOOD.

Today, nothing is more important then I feel good.

3
Write that here:

_____

_____

_____

_____

_____

_____

_____

5
NOTICE HOW THE SUN CAME UP AND THINGS ARE ALWAYS IN MOTION.

4
Close your eyes and see yourself aligning with source, blending into one.
Thank this constant focus upon you.

6
Feel and give thanks for the abundance of well-being all around.
For a full minute.

What 4 things would I like to turn over to the Universe to take care of for me today?

1._____

2._____

3._____

4._____

When you stop looking for the desired manifestation,
you learn that the feeling grows and carries you to the destination.

Write what things you intend to do today
and how you intend to feel as you accomplish these things.

1._____Feeling_____

2._____Feeling_____

3._____Feeling_____

4._____Feeling_____

I look forward to enjoying a productive and fun day.

Pick one of these emotions you would like to use
as today's intended feeling.
Ease, Relaxed, Comfort
Write this feeling here:_____
Now say to yourself...

**1.
MY INTENTION IS TO
REMIND MYSELF
MANY TIMES
TODAY...**

FOCUSING ON THIS
FEELING OF_____
IS MY REAL
JOB FOR THE DAY.

**2.
MY CURRENT
CONDITIONS ARE
IRRELEVANT
BECAUSE...**

I'M CREATING AN
ENVIRONMENT THAT
IS CAUSING THEM TO
CHANGE.

**3.
NO MORE SNAPSHOTS
OF WHAT IS
OR FEELING HELPLESS.**

TODAY, I AM GOING
TO USE THIS EMOTION
AS MY BASE FEELING
THAT WILL EFFECT
FUTURE OUTCOMES.

Close your eyes again and reach for this intended feeing in
place of the feeling of current reality. Notice the softening
of your body as you aligning with source.

Write your chosen daily focused emotion reaching
for the feeling.

_____ _____ _____
_____ _____ _____
_____ _____ _____
_____ _____ _____

ASK YOURSELF MANY TIMES TODAY
"Is this the attracting vibration, I want the universe to respond to?"
If not, for the count of 10 long breaths in and
slowly letting them out.
Say and feel your chosen emotion in appreciation for the feeling.
It self-creates without any evidence needed.

Write 3 things you would be interested in seeing that just for fun but
you are not worried about when.

_____
_____
_____

Let the universe show you these things in playful and exciting ways.

A THOUGHT REACHES A COMBUSTION POINT AT 16 SECONDS.

VIBRATIONAL CASH

A FULL 68 SECONDS ARE EQUIVALENT TO 2 MILLION MAN-HOURS.

Spend Your Vibrational Cash on one thing a day. If wanting a big ticket item slowly pay it off. This will make it more real for you.

The longer you spend feeling like the recipient of this desire the closer you are in being a match to it.

Focus on how it feels to buy this desire and the satisfaction attached within having it. Write about that satisfaction.

Close your eyes again and reach for the first thing that pops into your mind. No matter what the price tag is, big and small creations are all the same. Learn to start treating them all equal.

VIBRATIONAL CASH

DATE

PAY TO THE ORDER OF

5,000.00

IN YOUR CURRENCY

LIVE THE EXPERIENCE IN THE NOW

FOR _____

SIGN NAME HERE

_____
_____
_____
_____
_____
_____
_____
_____
_____

ASK, BELIEVE,
RECEIVE

ASK

What are ready to take the vibrational journey to?
By asking for this desire it means you are creating a gap and your job is to close it.

BELIEVE/SOURCE

THE MINUTE YOU ASK, IT IS DONE VIBRATIONALLY COMPLETE AND 99.99% DONE PHYSICALLY

RECEIVE:

Create a momentum in belief by feeling it is yours for 20 second, snap shots at a time. Focusing only on feeling not image.

If you hold an emotion as the desire. You no longer are creating an impossibility. The shift from in the future having the desire becomes felt in the present moment, and you will notice the tension has left the solar plexus as you do this.
At this moment you are able to isolate the components of the desire even without having the desire. You become expectant, Being expectant is a very high frequency, and it is one step away from the manifestation to occur.

What do you feel ready to change in your life.
By asking you are now saying "I will deliberately start creating this climate to close the gap.
I am aware of my part in how long the manifestation will take.

_____
_____
_____
_____
_____

Source has now become this vibrationally.
Your work is to create a mimicking or matching vibration.

Faith is created by reaching for the feeling and trusting the manifestation will follow.
Start now creating the feeling it is done by using small 20-second Virtual Realities while conjuring the emotions.
The idea is to preserve the focus that feels good longer, so you can match the frequency and enjoy the pleasures it provides in feelings.
Always leave the imagination
play through, if you feel anything but enjoyment.

POSITIVE ASPECTS

Appreciation is one of the highest vibrations you can use to shift how you are feeling.
It will build momentum fast and create an overall positive experience.
Even when you are in the worst of moods, if you focus on the parts that
you are appreciative for you will begin to start a new point of attraction.

I APPRECIATE YOU!
PERSON
NAME:
WHY?

_____
_____
_____
_____
_____

I APPRECIATE THE
BEAUTY FOUND HERE.
PLACE:
WHY?

_____
_____
_____
_____
_____

I APPRECIATE THE
BEAUTY FOUND HERE.
PLACE:
WHY?

_____
_____
_____
_____
_____

I APPRECIATE YOU!
PERSON
NAME:
WHY?

_____
_____
_____
_____
_____

I APPRECIATE HAVING
ACCESS TO THIS.
THING:
WHY?

_____
_____
_____
_____
_____

WHAT I LOVE ABOUT
THE WEATHER:
WHY?

_____
_____
_____
_____
_____

I APPRECIATE YOU!
PERSON
NAME:
WHY?

_____
_____
_____
_____

I APPRECIATE HAVING
ACCESS TO THIS.
THING:
WHY?

_____
_____
_____
_____

WHAT I LOVE ABOUT..
WHY?

_____
_____
_____
_____

POSITIVE
ASPECTS

Focus on anything and everything. Saying "thank you"
Creates more things to be thankful for.

I AM THANKFUL FOR: *WHY?*

_____
_____
_____
_____
_____

I AM THANKFUL FOR: *WHY?*

_____
_____
_____
_____
_____

I AM THANKFUL FOR: *WHY?*

_____
_____
_____
_____
_____

I AM THANKFUL FOR: *WHY?*

_____
_____
_____
_____
_____

I AM THANKFUL FOR: *WHY?*

_____
_____
_____
_____
_____

I AM THANKFUL FOR: *WHY?*

_____
_____
_____
_____
_____

I AM THANKFUL FOR: *WHY?*

_____
_____
_____
_____
_____

I AM THANKFUL FOR: *WHY?*

_____
_____
_____
_____
_____

I AM THANKFUL FOR: *WHY?*

_____
_____
_____
_____
_____

FOODS
yum! WHAT MY BODY ENJOYED TODAY

_____

_____

_____

_____

_____

_____

WATER INTAKE ✓
AM I HYDRATED?

GET PHYSICAL
WHAT MOVEMENT DID MY BODY ENJOY TODAY

_____

_____

_____

_____

_____

MEDITATION

SPEND 15 MINS FOCUSING ON REPETITIVE SOUND. THE MORE BORING IT IS THE BETTER.

A TO Z

WRITE WORDS FROM A TO Z FEELING FOR THEM AS YOU WRITE THEM MAKE UP WORDS IF YOU CANT THINK OF ONE.

A_____ B_____ C_____ D_____

E_____ F_____ G_____ H_____

I_____ J_____ K_____ L_____

M_____ N_____ O_____ P_____

Q_____ R_____ S_____ T_____

U_____ V_____ W_____ X_____

Y_____ Z_____

Am I match ____
If I am feeling ease and comfort in this moment then I am.
I will sit in the feeling of satisfaction at focusing on these emotions right now.

1   SIT FOR ONE MINUTE BREATHING

Focus on holding a smile while taking in long and deep breaths in and slowly letting them out. Relax your body and feel the comfort of where you sit.

2 REMIND YOURSELF HOW IMPORTANT IT IS TO FEEL GOOD.

Today, nothing is more important then I feel good.

3
Write that here:

_____
_____
_____
_____
_____
_____

4
Close your eyes and see yourself aligning with source, blending into one.
Thank this constant focus upon you.

5
NOTICE HOW THE SUN CAME UP AND THINGS ARE ALWAYS IN MOTION.

6
Feel and give thanks for the abundance of well-being all around.
For a full minute.

What 4 things would I like to turn over to the Universe to take care of for me today?

1. _____
2. _____
3. _____
4. _____

When you stop looking for the desired manifestation, you learn that the feeling grows and carries you to the destination.

Write what things you intend to do today and how you intend to feel as you accomplish these things.

1. _____ Feeling _____
2. _____ Feeling _____
3. _____ Feeling _____
4. _____ Feeling _____

I look forward to enjoying a productive and fun day.

Pick one of these emotions you would like to use
as today's intended feeling.
Ease, Relaxed, Comfort
Write this feeling here:_____
Now say to yourself...

**1.
MY INTENTION IS TO
REMIND MYSELF
MANY TIMES
TODAY...**

FOCUSING ON THIS
FEELING OF_____
IS MY REAL
JOB FOR THE DAY.

**2.
MY CURRENT
CONDITIONS ARE
IRRELEVANT
BECAUSE...**

I'M CREATING AN
ENVIRONMENT THAT
IS CAUSING THEM TO
CHANGE.

**3.
NO MORE SNAPSHOTS
OF WHAT IS
OR FEELING HELPLESS.**

TODAY, I AM GOING
TO USE THIS EMOTION
AS MY BASE FEELING
THAT WILL EFFECT
FUTURE OUTCOMES.

Close your eyes again and reach for this intended feeing in
place of the feeling of current reality. Notice the softening
of your body as you aligning with source.

$\longleftrightarrow$

Write your chosen daily focused emotion reaching
for the feeling.

_____ _____ _____
_____ _____ _____
_____ _____ _____
_____ _____ _____

ASK YOURSELF MANY TIMES TODAY
"Is this the attracting vibration, I want the universe to respond to?"
If not, for the count of 10 long breaths in and
slowly letting them out.
Say and feel your chosen emotion in appreciation for the feeling.
It self-creates without any evidence needed.

Write 3 things you would be interested in seeing that just for fun but
you are not worried about when.

_____
_____
_____

Let the universe show you these things in playful and exciting ways.

A THOUGHT REACHES A COMBUSTION POINT AT 16 SECONDS.

Spend Your Vibrational Cash on one thing a day. If wanting a big ticket item slowly pay it off. This will make it more real for you.

VIBRATIONAL CASH

The longer you spend feeling like the recipient of this desire the closer you are in being a match to it.

A FULL 68 SECONDS ARE EQUIVALENT TO 2 MILLION MAN-HOURS.

Focus on how it feels to buy this desire and the satisfaction attached within having it. Write about that satisfaction.

Close your eyes again and reach for the first thing that pops into your mind. No matter what the price tag is, big and small creations are all the same. Learn to start treating them all equal.

VIBRATIONALCASH

DATE _____

PAY TO THE ORDER OF

5,000.00

IN YOUR CURRENCY

LIVE THE EXPERIENCE IN THE NOW

FOR _____

SIGN NAME HERE

_____
_____
_____
_____
_____
_____
_____
_____
_____

ASK, BELIEVE,
RECEIVE

ASK

What are ready to take the vibrational journey to?
By asking for this desire it means you are creating a gap and your job is to close it.

BELIEVE/SOURCE

THE MINUTE YOU ASK, IT IS DONE VIBRATIONALLY COMPLETE AND 99.99% DONE PHYSICALLY

RECEIVE:

Create a momentum in belief by feeling it is yours for 20 second, snap shots at a time. Focusing only on feeling not image.

If you hold an emotion as the desire. You no longer are creating an impossibility. The shift from in the future having the desire becomes felt in the present moment, and you will notice the tension has left the solar plexus as you do this.
At this moment you are able to isolate the components of the desire even without having the desire. You become expectant, Being expectant is a very high frequency, and it is one step away from the manifestation to occur.

What do you feel ready to change in your life.
By asking you are now saying "I will deliberately start creating this climate to close the gap.
I am aware of my part in how long the manifestation will take.

_____
_____
_____
_____
_____

Source has now become this vibrationally.
Your work is to create a mimicking or matching vibration.

Faith is created by reaching for the feeling and trusting the manifestation will follow.
Start now creating the feeling it is done by using small 20-second Virtual Realities while conjuring the emotions.
The idea is to preserve the focus that feels good longer, so you can match the frequency and enjoy the pleasures it provides in feelings.
Always leave the imagination play through, if you feel anything but enjoyment.

POSITIVE ASPECTS

Appreciation is one of the highest vibrations you can use to shift how you are feeling.
It will build momentum fast and create an overall positive experience.
Even when you are in the worst of moods, if you focus on the parts that
you are appreciative for you will begin to start a new point of attraction.

I APPRECIATE YOU!
PERSON
NAME: *WHY?*

_____
_____
_____
_____
_____

I APPRECIATE THE
BEAUTY FOUND HERE.
PLACE: *WHY?*

_____
_____
_____
_____
_____

I APPRECIATE THE
BEAUTY FOUND HERE.
PLACE: *WHY?*

_____
_____
_____
_____
_____

I APPRECIATE YOU!
PERSON
NAME: *WHY?*

_____
_____
_____
_____
_____

I APPRECIATE HAVING
ACCESS TO THIS.
THING: *WHY?*

_____
_____
_____
_____
_____

WHAT I LOVE ABOUT
THE WEATHER: *WHY?*

_____
_____
_____
_____
_____

I APPRECIATE YOU!
PERSON
NAME: *WHY?*

_____
_____
_____
_____
_____

I APPRECIATE HAVING
ACCESS TO THIS.
THING: *WHY?*

_____
_____
_____
_____
_____

WHAT I LOVE ABOUT..
                        WHY?

_____
_____
_____
_____
_____

POSITIVE
ASPECTS

Focus on anything and everything. Saying "thank you"
Creates more things to be thankful for.

I AM THANKFUL FOR: *WHY?*

_____
_____
_____
_____
_____

I AM THANKFUL FOR: *WHY?*

_____
_____
_____
_____
_____

I AM THANKFUL FOR: *WHY?*

_____
_____
_____
_____
_____

I AM THANKFUL FOR: *WHY?*

_____
_____
_____
_____
_____

I AM THANKFUL FOR: *WHY?*

_____
_____
_____
_____
_____

I AM THANKFUL FOR: *WHY?*

_____
_____
_____
_____
_____

I AM THANKFUL FOR: *WHY?*

_____
_____
_____
_____
_____

I AM THANKFUL FOR: *WHY?*

_____
_____
_____
_____
_____

I AM THANKFUL FOR: *WHY?*

_____
_____
_____
_____
_____

FOODS
yum! WHAT MY BODY ENJOYED TODAY

_____

_____

_____

_____

_____

_____

_____

WATER INTAKE
AM I HYDRATED?

GET PHYSICAL
WHAT MOVEMENT DID MY BODY ENJOY TODAY

_____

_____

_____

_____

_____

MEDITATION

SPEND 15 MINS FOCUSING ON REPETITIVE SOUND. THE MORE BORING IT IS THE BETTER.

A TO Z

WRITE WORDS FROM A TO Z FEELING FOR THEM AS YOU WRITE THEM MAKE UP WORDS IF YOU CANT THINK OF ONE.

A_____ B_____ C_____ D_____

E_____ F_____ G_____ H_____

I_____ J_____ K_____ L_____

M_____ N_____ O_____ P_____

Q_____ R_____ S_____ T_____

U_____ V_____ W_____ X_____

Y_____ Z_____

Am I match _____
If I am feeling ease and comfort in this moment then I am.
I will sit in the feeling of satisfaction at focusing on these emotions right now.

1 SIT FOR ONE MINUTE BREATHING

Focus on holding a smile while taking in long and deep breaths in and slowly letting them out. Relax your body and feel the comfort of where you sit.

2 REMIND YOURSELF HOW IMPORTANT IT IS TO FEEL GOOD.

Today, nothing is more important then I feel good.

3

Write that here:

_____

_____

_____

_____

_____

_____

_____

5 NOTICE HOW THE SUN CAME UP AND THINGS ARE ALWAYS IN MOTION.

4

Close your eyes and see yourself aligning with source, blending into one. Thank this constant focus upon you.

6

Feel and give thanks for the abundance of well-being all around. For a full minute.

What 4 things would I like to turn over to the Universe to take care of for me today?

1._____

2._____

3._____

4._____

When you stop looking for the desired manifestation, you learn that the feeling grows and carries you to the destination.

Write what things you intend to do today and how you intend to feel as you accomplish these things.

1._____Feeling_____

2._____Feeling_____

3._____Feeling_____

4._____Feeling_____

I look forward to enjoying a productive and fun day.

Pick one of these emotions you would like to use
as today's intended feeling.
Ease, Relaxed, Comfort
Write this feeling here:_____
Now say to yourself...

**1.
MY INTENTION IS TO
REMIND MYSELF
MANY TIMES
TODAY...**

FOCUSING ON THIS
FEELING OF_____
IS MY REAL
JOB FOR THE DAY.

**2.
MY CURRENT
CONDITIONS ARE
IRRELEVANT
BECAUSE...**

I'M CREATING AN
ENVIRONMENT THAT
IS CAUSING THEM TO
CHANGE.

**3.
NO MORE SNAPSHOTS
OF WHAT IS
OR FEELING HELPLESS.**

TODAY, I AM GOING
TO USE THIS EMOTION
AS MY BASE FEELING
THAT WILL EFFECT
FUTURE OUTCOMES.

Close your eyes again and reach for this intended feeing in
place of the feeling of current reality. Notice the softening
of your body as you aligning with source.

Write your chosen daily focused emotion reaching
for the feeling.

_____ _____ _____
_____ _____ _____
_____ _____ _____
_____ _____ _____

ASK YOURSELF MANY TIMES TODAY
"Is this the attracting vibration, I want the universe to respond to?"
If not, for the count of 10 long breaths in and
slowly letting them out.
Say and feel your chosen emotion in appreciation for the feeling.
It self-creates without any evidence needed.

Write 3 things you would be interested in seeing that just for fun but
you are not worried about when.

_____
_____
_____

Let the universe show you these things in playful and exciting ways.

A THOUGHT REACHES A COMBUSTION POINT AT 16 SECONDS.

VIBRATIONAL CASH

A FULL 68 SECONDS ARE EQUIVALENT TO 2 MILLION MAN-HOURS.

Spend Your Vibrational Cash on one thing a day. If wanting a big ticket item slowly pay it off. This will make it more real for you.

The longer you spend feeling like the recipient of this desire the closer you are in being a match to it.

Focus on how it feels to buy this desire and the satisfaction attached within having it. Write about that satisfaction.

Close your eyes again and reach for the first thing that pops into your mind. No matter what the price tag is, big and small creations are all the same. Learn to start treating them all equal.

VIBRATIONALCASH

DATE _____

PAY TO THE ORDER OF _____

5,000.00

IN YOUR CURRENCY

LIVE THE EXPERIENCE IN THE NOW

FOR _____

SIGN NAME HERE

_____
_____
_____
_____
_____
_____
_____
_____
_____

ASK, BELIEVE,
RECEIVE

ASK

What are ready to take the vibrational journey to?
By asking for this desire it means you are creating a gap and your job is to close it.

BELIEVE/SOURCE

THE MINUTE YOU ASK, IT IS DONE VIBRATIONALLY COMPLETE AND 99.99% DONE PHYSICALLY

RECEIVE:

Create a momentum in belief by feeling it is yours for 20 second, snap shots at a time. Focusing only on feeling not image.

If you hold an emotion as the desire. You no longer are creating an impossibility. The shift from in the future having the desire becomes felt in the present moment, and you will notice the tension has left the solar plexus as you do this.
At this moment you are able to isolate the components of the desire even without having the desire. You become expectant, Being expectant is a very high frequency, and it is one step away from the manifestation to occur.

What do you feel ready to change in your life.
By asking you are now saying "I will deliberately start creating this climate to close the gap. I am aware of my part in how long the manifestation will take.

_____

_____

_____

_____

_____

Source has now become this vibrationally.
Your work is to create a mimicking or matching vibration.

Faith is created by reaching for the feeling and trusting the manifestation will follow.
Start now creating the feeling it is done by using small 20-second Virtual Realities while conjuring the emotions.
The idea is to preserve the focus that feels good longer, so you can match the frequency and enjoy the pleasures it provides in feelings.
Always leave the imagination play through, if you feel anything but enjoyment.

POSITIVE ASPECTS

Appreciation is one of the highest vibrations you can use to shift how you are feeling. It will build momentum fast and create an overall positive experience. Even when you are in the worst of moods, if you focus on the parts that you are appreciative for you will begin to start a new point of attraction.

I APPRECIATE YOU!
PERSON
NAME: *WHY?*

_____
_____
_____
_____
_____

I APPRECIATE THE BEAUTY FOUND HERE.
PLACE: *WHY?*

_____
_____
_____
_____

I APPRECIATE THE BEAUTY FOUND HERE.
PLACE: *WHY?*

_____
_____
_____
_____

I APPRECIATE YOU!
PERSON
NAME: *WHY?*

_____
_____
_____
_____

I APPRECIATE HAVING ACCESS TO THIS.
THING: *WHY?*

_____
_____
_____

WHAT I LOVE ABOUT THE WEATHER: *WHY?*

_____
_____
_____
_____

I APPRECIATE YOU!
PERSON
NAME: *WHY?*

_____
_____
_____
_____

I APPRECIATE HAVING ACCESS TO THIS.
THING: *WHY?*

_____
_____
_____
_____

WHAT I LOVE ABOUT.. *WHY?*

_____
_____
_____
_____

POSITIVE
ASPECTS

Focus on anything and everything. Saying "thank you"
Creates more things to be thankful for.

I AM THANKFUL
FOR: *WHY?*

_____
_____
_____
_____
_____

I AM THANKFUL
FOR: *WHY?*

_____
_____
_____
_____
_____

I AM THANKFUL
FOR: *WHY?*

_____
_____
_____
_____
_____

I AM THANKFUL
FOR: *WHY?*

_____
_____
_____
_____
_____

I AM THANKFUL
FOR: *WHY?*

_____
_____
_____
_____
_____

I AM THANKFUL *WHY?*
FOR:

_____
_____
_____
_____
_____

I AM THANKFUL
FOR: *WHY?*

_____
_____
_____
_____
_____

I AM THANKFUL
FOR: *WHY?*

_____
_____
_____
_____
_____

I AM THANKFUL
FOR: *WHY?*

_____
_____
_____
_____
_____

FOODS
yum! WHAT MY BODY
ENJOYED TODAY

_____
_____
_____
_____
_____
_____

WATER INTAKE
AM I HYDRATED? ✓

GET PHYSICAL
WHAT MOVEMENT DID MY BODY ENJOY TODAY

_____
_____
_____
_____
_____

MEDITATION

SPEND 15 MINS FOCUSING
ON REPETITIVE SOUND.
THE MORE BORING IT IS THE
BETTER.

A TO Z

WRITE WORDS FROM A TO Z
FEELING FOR THEM AS YOU
WRITE THEM MAKE UP
WORDS IF YOU CANT THINK
OF ONE.

A_____ B_____ C_____ D_____

E_____ F_____ G_____ H_____

I_____ J_____ K_____ L_____

M_____ N_____ O_____ P_____

Q_____ R_____ S_____ T_____

U_____ V_____ W_____ X_____

Y_____ Z_____

Am I match ____
If I am feeling ease and comfort in this moment then I am.
I will sit in the feeling of satisfaction at focusing on these emotions right now.

1 SIT FOR ONE MINUTE BREATHING

Focus on holding a smile while taking in long and deep breaths in and slowly letting them out. Relax your body and feel the comfort of where you sit.

2 REMIND YOURSELF HOW IMPORTANT IT IS TO FEEL GOOD.

Today, nothing is more important then I feel good.

3 *Write that here:*

_____
_____
_____
_____
_____
_____

4

Close your eyes and see yourself aligning with source, blending into one.
Thank this constant focus upon you.

5 NOTICE HOW THE SUN CAME UP AND THINGS ARE ALWAYS IN MOTION.

6

Feel and give thanks for the abundance of well-being all around.
For a full minute.

What 4 things would I like to turn over to the Universe to take care of for me today?

1._____
2._____
3._____
4._____

When you stop looking for the desired manifestation, you learn that the feeling grows and carries you to the destination.

Write what things you intend to do today and how you intend to feel as you accomplish these things.

1._____Feeling_____
2._____Feeling_____
3._____Feeling_____
4._____Feeling_____

I look forward to enjoying a productive and fun day.

Pick one of these emotions you would like to use
as today's intended feeling.
Ease, Relaxed, Comfort
Write this feeling here:_____
Now say to yourself...

1.
MY INTENTION IS TO REMIND MYSELF MANY TIMES TODAY...

FOCUSING ON THIS FEELING OF_____ IS MY REAL JOB FOR THE DAY.

2.
MY CURRENT CONDITIONS ARE IRRELEVANT BECAUSE...

I'M CREATING AN ENVIRONMENT THAT IS CAUSING THEM TO CHANGE.

3.
NO MORE SNAPSHOTS OF WHAT IS OR FEELING HELPLESS.

TODAY, I AM GOING TO USE THIS EMOTION AS MY BASE FEELING THAT WILL EFFECT FUTURE OUTCOMES.

Close your eyes again and reach for this intended feeing in place of the feeling of current reality. Notice the softening of your body as you aligning with source.

Write your chosen daily focused emotion reaching for the feeling.

_____ _____ _____
_____ _____ _____
_____ _____ _____
_____ _____ _____

ASK YOURSELF MANY TIMES TODAY
"Is this the attracting vibration, I want the universe to respond to?"
If not, for the count of 10 long breaths in and
slowly letting them out.
Say and feel your chosen emotion in appreciation for the feeling.
It self-creates without any evidence needed.

Write 3 things you would be interested in seeing that just for fun but you are not worried about when.

_____
_____
_____

Let the universe show you these things in playful and exciting ways.

A THOUGHT REACHES A COMBUSTION POINT AT 16 SECONDS.

VIBRATIONAL CASH

A FULL 68 SECONDS ARE EQUIVALENT TO 2 MILLION MAN-HOURS.

Spend Your Vibrational Cash on one thing a day. If wanting a big ticket item slowly pay it off. This will make it more real for you.

The longer you spend feeling like the recipient of this desire the closer you are in being a match to it.

Focus on how it feels to buy this desire and the satisfaction attached within having it. Write about that satisfaction.

Close your eyes again and reach for the first thing that pops into your mind. No matter what the price tag is, big and small creations are all the same. Learn to start treating them all equal.

VIBRATIONALCASH

DATE _____

PAY TO
THE ORDER OF _____

5,000.00

IN YOUR CURRENCY

LIVE THE EXPERIENCE IN THE NOW

FOR _____

SIGN NAME HERE

_____
_____
_____
_____
_____
_____
_____
_____
_____
_____

ASK, BELIEVE, RECEIVE

ASK

What are ready to take the vibrational journey to?
By asking for this desire it means you are creating a gap and your job is to close it.

BELIEVE/SOURCE

THE MINUTE YOU ASK, IT IS DONE VIBRATIONALLY COMPLETE AND 99.99% DONE PHYSICALLY

RECEIVE:

Create a momentum in belief by feeling it is yours for 20 second, snap shots at a time. Focusing only on feeling not image.

If you hold an emotion as the desire. You no longer are creating an impossibility. The shift from in the future having the desire becomes felt in the present moment, and you will notice the tension has left the solar plexus as you do this.
At this moment you are able to isolate the components of the desire even without having the desire. You become expectant, Being expectant is a very high frequency, and it is one step away from the manifestation to occur.

What do you feel ready to change in your life.
By asking you are now saying "I will deliberately start creating this climate to close the gap. I am aware of my part in how long the manifestation will take.

_____
_____
_____
_____
_____

Source has now become this vibrationally.
Your work is to create a mimicking or matching vibration.

Faith is created by reaching for the feeling and trusting the manifestation will follow.
Start now creating the feeling it is done by using small 20-second Virtual Realities while conjuring the emotions.
The idea is to preserve the focus that feels good longer, so you can match the frequency and enjoy the pleasures it provides in feelings.
Always leave the imagination play through, if you feel anything but enjoyment.

POSITIVE ASPECTS

Appreciation is one of the highest vibrations you can use to shift how you are feeling. It will build momentum fast and create an overall positive experience. Even when you are in the worst of moods, if you focus on the parts that you are appreciative for you will begin to start a new point of attraction.

I APPRECIATE YOU!
PERSON
NAME: *WHY?*

_____
_____
_____
_____
_____

I APPRECIATE THE BEAUTY FOUND HERE.
PLACE: *WHY?*

_____
_____
_____
_____
_____

I APPRECIATE THE BEAUTY FOUND HERE.
PLACE: *WHY?*

_____
_____
_____
_____
_____

I APPRECIATE YOU!
PERSON
NAME: *WHY?*

_____
_____
_____
_____
_____

I APPRECIATE HAVING ACCESS TO THIS.
THING: *WHY?*

_____
_____
_____
_____
_____

WHAT I LOVE ABOUT THE WEATHER: *WHY?*

_____
_____
_____
_____
_____

I APPRECIATE YOU!
PERSON
NAME: *WHY?*

_____
_____
_____
_____
_____

I APPRECIATE HAVING ACCESS TO THIS.
THING: *WHY?*

_____
_____
_____
_____
_____

WHAT I LOVE ABOUT..
                    WHY?

_____
_____
_____
_____
_____

POSITIVE
ASPECTS

Focus on anything and everything. Saying "thank you"
Creates more things to be thankful for.

I AM THANKFUL FOR: *WHY?*

_____
_____
_____
_____
_____

I AM THANKFUL FOR: *WHY?*

_____
_____
_____
_____
_____

I AM THANKFUL FOR: *WHY?*

_____
_____
_____
_____
_____

I AM THANKFUL FOR: *WHY?*

_____
_____
_____
_____
_____

I AM THANKFUL FOR: *WHY?*

_____
_____
_____
_____
_____

I AM THANKFUL FOR: *WHY?*

_____
_____
_____
_____
_____

I AM THANKFUL FOR: *WHY?*

_____
_____
_____
_____
_____

I AM THANKFUL FOR: *WHY?*

_____
_____
_____
_____
_____

I AM THANKFUL FOR: *WHY?*

_____
_____
_____
_____
_____

FOODS
yum! WHAT MY BODY ENJOYED TODAY

_____
_____
_____
_____
_____
_____

WATER INTAKE ✓
AM I HYDRATED?

GET PHYSICAL
WHAT MOVEMENT DID MY BODY ENJOY TODAY

_____
_____
_____
_____
_____

MEDITATION
SPEND 15 MINS FOCUSING ON REPETITIVE SOUND. THE MORE BORING IT IS THE BETTER.

A TO Z
WRITE WORDS FROM A TO Z FEELING FOR THEM AS YOU WRITE THEM MAKE UP WORDS IF YOU CANT THINK OF ONE.

A_____ B_____ C_____ D_____

E_____ F_____ G_____ H_____

I_____ J_____ K_____ L_____

M_____ N_____ O_____ P_____

Q_____ R_____ S_____ T_____

U_____ V_____ W_____ X_____

Y_____ Z_____

Am I match ____
If I am feeling ease and comfort in this moment then I am.
I will sit in the feeling of satisfaction at focusing on these emotions right now.

1 SIT FOR ONE MINUTE BREATHING

Focus on holding a smile while taking in long and deep breaths in and slowly letting them out. Relax your body and feel the comfort of where you sit.

2 REMIND YOURSELF HOW IMPORTANT IT IS TO FEEL GOOD.

Today, nothing is more important then I feel good.

3 Write that here:

_____

_____

_____

_____

_____

_____

4

Close your eyes and see yourself aligning with source, blending into one.
Thank this constant focus upon you.

5 NOTICE HOW THE SUN CAME UP AND THINGS ARE ALWAYS IN MOTION.

6

Feel and give thanks for the abundance of well-being all around.
For a full minute.

What 4 things would I like to turn over to the Universe to take care of for me today?

1._____

2._____

3._____

4._____

When you stop looking for the desired manifestation, you learn that the feeling grows and carries you to the destination.

Write what things you intend to do today
and how you intend to feel as you accomplish these things.

1._____Feeling_____

2._____Feeling_____

3._____Feeling_____

4._____Feeling_____

I look forward to enjoying a productive and fun day.

Pick one of these emotions you would like to use
as today's intended feeling.
Ease, Relaxed, Comfort
Write this feeling here:_____
Now say to yourself...

1.
MY INTENTION IS TO REMIND MYSELF MANY TIMES TODAY...

FOCUSING ON THIS FEELING OF_____ IS MY REAL JOB FOR THE DAY.

2.
MY CURRENT CONDITIONS ARE IRRELEVANT BECAUSE...

I'M CREATING AN ENVIRONMENT THAT IS CAUSING THEM TO CHANGE.

3.
NO MORE SNAPSHOTS OF WHAT IS OR FEELING HELPLESS.

TODAY, I AM GOING TO USE THIS EMOTION AS MY BASE FEELING THAT WILL EFFECT FUTURE OUTCOMES.

Close your eyes again and reach for this intended feeing in place of the feeling of current reality. Notice the softening of your body as you aligning with source.

Write your chosen daily focused emotion reaching for the feeling.

_____ _____ _____
_____ _____ _____
_____ _____ _____
_____ _____ _____

ASK YOURSELF MANY TIMES TODAY
"Is this the attracting vibration, I want the universe to respond to?"
If not, for the count of 10 long breaths in and
slowly letting them out.
Say and feel your chosen emotion in appreciation for the feeling.
It self-creates without any evidence needed.

Write 3 things you would be interested in seeing that just for fun but you are not worried about when.

_____
_____
_____

Let the universe show you these things in playful and exciting ways.

A THOUGHT REACHES A COMBUSTION POINT AT 16 SECONDS.

VIBRATIONAL CASH

A FULL 68 SECONDS ARE EQUIVALENT TO 2 MILLION MAN-HOURS.

Spend Your Vibrational Cash on one thing a day. If wanting a big ticket item slowly pay it off. This will make it more real for you.

The longer you spend feeling like the recipient of this desire the closer you are in being a match to it.

Focus on how it feels to buy this desire and the satisfaction attached within having it. Write about that satisfaction.

Close your eyes again and reach for the first thing that pops into your mind. No matter what the price tag is, big and small creations are all the same. Learn to start treating them all equal.

VIBRATIONAL CASH

DATE

PAY TO THE ORDER OF

5,000.00

IN YOUR CURRENCY

LIVE THE EXPERIENCE IN THE NOW

FOR

SIGN NAME HERE

_____
_____
_____
_____
_____
_____
_____
_____
_____
_____

ASK, BELIEVE,
RECEIVE

ASK

What are ready to take the vibrational journey to?
By asking for this desire it means you are creating a gap and your job is to close it.

BELIEVE/SOURCE

THE MINUTE YOU ASK, IT IS DONE VIBRATIONALLY COMPLETE AND 99.99% DONE PHYSICALLY

RECEIVE:

Create a momentum in belief by feeling it is yours for 20 second, snap shots at a time. Focusing only on feeling not image.

If you hold an emotion as the desire. You no longer are creating an impossibility. The shift from in the future having the desire becomes felt in the present moment, and you will notice the tension has left the solar plexus as you do this.
At this moment you are able to isolate the components of the desire even without having the desire. You become expectant, Being expectant is a very high frequency, and it is one step away from the manifestation to occur.

⬅ ➡

What do you feel ready to change in your life.
By asking you are now saying "I will deliberately start creating this climate to close the gap. I am aware of my part in how long the manifestation will take.

_____
_____
_____
_____
_____

Source has now become this vibrationally.
Your work is to create a mimicking or matching vibration.

Faith is created by reaching for the feeling and trusting the manifestation will follow.
Start now creating the feeling it is done by using small 20-second Virtual Realities while conjuring the emotions.
The idea is to preserve the focus that feels good longer, so you can match the frequency and enjoy the pleasures it provides in feelings.
Always leave the imagination
play through, if you feel anything but enjoyment.

POSITIVE ASPECTS

Appreciation is one of the highest vibrations you can use to shift how you are feeling.
It will build momentum fast and create an overall positive experience.
Even when you are in the worst of moods, if you focus on the parts that
you are appreciative for you will begin to start a new point of attraction.

I APPRECIATE YOU!
PERSON
NAME: *WHY?*

_____
_____
_____
_____
_____

I APPRECIATE THE
BEAUTY FOUND HERE.
PLACE: *WHY?*

_____
_____
_____
_____
_____

I APPRECIATE THE
BEAUTY FOUND HERE.
PLACE: *WHY?*

_____
_____
_____
_____
_____

I APPRECIATE YOU!
PERSON
NAME: *WHY?*

_____
_____
_____
_____
_____

I APPRECIATE HAVING
ACCESS TO THIS.
THING: *WHY?*

_____
_____
_____
_____

WHAT I LOVE ABOUT
THE WEATHER: *WHY?*

_____
_____
_____
_____

I APPRECIATE YOU!
PERSON
NAME: *WHY?*

_____
_____
_____

I APPRECIATE HAVING
ACCESS TO THIS.
THING: *WHY?*

_____
_____
_____

WHAT I LOVE ABOUT..
                          WHY?

_____
_____
_____

POSITIVE
ASPECTS

Focus on anything and everything. Saying "thank you"
Creates more things to be thankful for.

I AM THANKFUL FOR: *WHY?*

_____
_____
_____
_____
_____

I AM THANKFUL FOR: *WHY?*

_____
_____
_____
_____
_____

I AM THANKFUL FOR: *WHY?*

_____
_____
_____
_____
_____

I AM THANKFUL FOR: *WHY?*

_____
_____
_____
_____
_____

I AM THANKFUL FOR: *WHY?*

_____
_____
_____
_____
_____

I AM THANKFUL FOR: *WHY?*

_____
_____
_____
_____
_____

I AM THANKFUL FOR: *WHY?*

_____
_____
_____
_____
_____

I AM THANKFUL FOR: *WHY?*

_____
_____
_____
_____
_____

I AM THANKFUL FOR: *WHY?*

_____
_____
_____
_____
_____

FOODS

yum! WHAT MY BODY ENJOYED TODAY

_____
_____
_____
_____
_____

WATER INTAKE

✓

AM I HYDRATED?

GET PHYSICAL

WHAT MOVEMENT DID MY BODY ENJOY TODAY

_____
_____
_____
_____

MEDITATION

SPEND 15 MINS FOCUSING ON REPETITIVE SOUND. THE MORE BORING IT IS THE BETTER.

A TO Z

WRITE WORDS FROM A TO Z FEELING FOR THEM AS YOU WRITE THEM MAKE UP WORDS IF YOU CANT THINK OF ONE.

A_____ B_____ C_____ D_____

E_____ F_____ G_____ H_____

I_____ J_____ K_____ L_____

M_____ N_____ O_____ P_____

Q_____ R_____ S_____ T_____

U_____ V_____ W_____ X_____

Y_____ Z_____

Am I match ____
If I am feeling ease and comfort in this moment then I am.
I will sit in the feeling of satisfaction at focusing on these emotions right now.

1 SIT FOR ONE MINUTE BREATHING

Focus on holding a smile while taking in long and deep breaths in and slowly letting them out. Relax your body and feel the comfort of where you sit.

2 REMIND YOURSELF HOW IMPORTANT IT IS TO FEEL GOOD.

Today, nothing is more important then I feel good.

3

Write that here:

_____

_____

_____

_____

_____

_____

5 NOTICE HOW THE SUN CAME UP AND THINGS ARE ALWAYS IN MOTION.

4

Close your eyes and see yourself aligning with source, blending into one. Thank this constant focus upon you.

6

Feel and give thanks for the abundance of well-being all around. For a full minute.

What 4 things would I like to turn over to the Universe to take care of for me today?

1._____

2._____

3._____

4._____

When you stop looking for the desired manifestation, you learn that the feeling grows and carries you to the destination.

Write what things you intend to do today and how you intend to feel as you accomplish these things.

1._____Feeling_____

2._____Feeling_____

3._____Feeling_____

4._____Feeling_____

I look forward to enjoying a productive and fun day.

Pick one of these emotions you would like to use
as today's intended feeling.
Ease, Relaxed, Comfort
Write this feeling here:_____
Now say to yourself...

1.
MY INTENTION IS TO REMIND MYSELF MANY TIMES TODAY...

FOCUSING ON THIS FEELING OF_____ IS MY REAL JOB FOR THE DAY.

2.
MY CURRENT CONDITIONS ARE IRRELEVANT BECAUSE...

I'M CREATING AN ENVIRONMENT THAT IS CAUSING THEM TO CHANGE.

3.
NO MORE SNAPSHOTS OF WHAT IS OR FEELING HELPLESS.

TODAY, I AM GOING TO USE THIS EMOTION AS MY BASE FEELING THAT WILL EFFECT FUTURE OUTCOMES.

Close your eyes again and reach for this intended feeing in place of the feeling of current reality. Notice the softening of your body as you aligning with source.

Write your chosen daily focused emotion reaching for the feeling.

_____ _____ _____
_____ _____ _____
_____ _____ _____
_____ _____ _____

ASK YOURSELF MANY TIMES TODAY
"Is this the attracting vibration, I want the universe to respond to?"
If not, for the count of 10 long breaths in and
slowly letting them out.
Say and feel your chosen emotion in appreciation for the feeling.
It self-creates without any evidence needed.

Write 3 things you would be interested in seeing that just for fun but you are not worried about when.

_____
_____
_____

Let the universe show you these things in playful and exciting ways.

A THOUGHT REACHES A COMBUSTION POINT AT 16 SECONDS.

VIBRATIONAL CASH

A FULL 68 SECONDS ARE EQUIVALENT TO 2 MILLION MAN-HOURS.

Spend Your Vibrational Cash on one thing a day. If wanting a big ticket item slowly pay it off. This will make it more real for you.

The longer you spend feeling like the recipient of this desire the closer you are in being a match to it.

Focus on how it feels to buy this desire and the satisfaction attached within having it. Write about that satisfaction.

Close your eyes again and reach for the first thing that pops into your mind. No matter what the price tag is, big and small creations are all the same. Learn to start treating them all equal.

VIBRATIONAL CASH

PAY TO THE ORDER OF

DATE

5,000.00

IN YOUR CURRENCY

LIVE THE EXPERIENCE IN THE NOW

FOR _____

SIGN NAME HERE

_____
_____
_____
_____
_____
_____
_____
_____
_____
_____

ASK, BELIEVE,
RECEIVE

ASK

What are ready to take the vibrational journey to?
By asking for this desire it means you are creating a gap and your job is to close it.

BELIEVE/SOURCE

THE MINUTE YOU ASK, IT IS DONE VIBRATIONALLY COMPLETE AND 99.99% DONE PHYSICALLY

RECEIVE:

Create a momentum in belief by feeling it is yours for 20 second, snap shots at a time. Focusing only on feeling not image.

If you hold an emotion as the desire. You no longer are creating an impossibility. The shift from in the future having the desire becomes felt in the present moment, and you will notice the tension has left the solar plexus as you do this.
At this moment you are able to isolate the components of the desire even without having the desire. You become expectant, Being expectant is a very high frequency, and it is one step away from the manifestation to occur.

What do you feel ready to change in your life.
By asking you are now saying "I will deliberately start creating this climate to close the gap.
I am aware of my part in how long the manifestation will take.

_____
_____
_____
_____
_____

Source has now become this vibrationally.
Your work is to create a mimicking or matching vibration.

Faith is created by reaching for the feeling and trusting the manifestation will follow.
Start now creating the feeling it is done by using small 20-second Virtual Realities while conjuring the emotions.
The idea is to preserve the focus that feels good longer, so you can match the frequency and enjoy the pleasures it provides in feelings.
Always leave the imagination play through, if you feel anything but enjoyment.

POSITIVE ASPECTS

Appreciation is one of the highest vibrations you can use to shift how you are feeling.
It will build momentum fast and create an overall positive experience.
Even when you are in the worst of moods, if you focus on the parts that
you are appreciative for you will begin to start a new point of attraction.

I APPRECIATE YOU!
PERSON
NAME: *WHY?*

_____
_____
_____
_____
_____

I APPRECIATE THE
BEAUTY FOUND HERE.
PLACE: *WHY?*

_____
_____
_____
_____
_____

I APPRECIATE THE
BEAUTY FOUND HERE.
PLACE: *WHY?*

_____
_____
_____
_____
_____

I APPRECIATE YOU!
PERSON
NAME: *WHY?*

_____
_____
_____
_____
_____

I APPRECIATE HAVING
ACCESS TO THIS.
THING: *WHY?*

_____
_____
_____
_____
_____

WHAT I LOVE ABOUT
THE WEATHER: *WHY?*

_____
_____
_____
_____
_____

I APPRECIATE YOU!
PERSON
NAME: *WHY?*

_____
_____
_____
_____

I APPRECIATE HAVING
ACCESS TO THIS.
THING: *WHY?*

_____
_____
_____
_____

WHAT I LOVE ABOUT..
WHY?

_____
_____
_____
_____

POSITIVE
ASPECTS

Focus on anything and everything. Saying "thank you"
Creates more things to be thankful for.

I AM THANKFUL FOR: *WHY?*

_____
_____
_____
_____
_____

I AM THANKFUL FOR: *WHY?*

_____
_____
_____
_____
_____

I AM THANKFUL FOR: *WHY?*

_____
_____
_____
_____
_____

I AM THANKFUL FOR: *WHY?*

_____
_____
_____
_____
_____

I AM THANKFUL FOR: *WHY?*

_____
_____
_____
_____
_____

I AM THANKFUL FOR: *WHY?*

_____
_____
_____
_____
_____

I AM THANKFUL FOR: *WHY?*

_____
_____
_____
_____
_____

I AM THANKFUL FOR: *WHY?*

_____
_____
_____
_____
_____

I AM THANKFUL FOR: *WHY?*

_____
_____
_____
_____
_____

FOODS

yum! WHAT MY BODY ENJOYED TODAY

_____

_____

_____

_____

_____

_____

_____

WATER INTAKE

✓

AM I HYDRATED?

GET PHYSICAL

WHAT MOVEMENT DID MY BODY ENJOY TODAY

_____

_____

_____

_____

_____

MEDITATION

SPEND 15 MINS FOCUSING ON REPETITIVE SOUND. THE MORE BORING IT IS THE BETTER.

A TO Z

WRITE WORDS FROM A TO Z FEELING FOR THEM AS YOU WRITE THEM MAKE UP WORDS IF YOU CANT THINK OF ONE.

A_____ B_____ C_____ D_____

E_____ F_____ G_____ H_____

I_____ J_____ K_____ L_____

M_____ N_____ O_____ P_____

Q_____ R_____ S_____ T_____

U_____ V_____ W_____ X_____

Y_____ Z_____

Am I match ____
If I am feeling ease and comfort in this moment then I am.
I will sit in the feeling of satisfaction at focusing on these emotions right now.

1 SIT FOR ONE MINUTE BREATHING

Focus on holding a smile while taking in long and deep breaths in and slowly letting them out. Relax your body and feel the comfort of where you sit.

2 REMIND YOURSELF HOW IMPORTANT IT IS TO FEEL GOOD.

Today, nothing is more important then I feel good.

3
Write that here:

_____
_____
_____
_____
_____
_____

5
NOTICE HOW THE SUN CAME UP AND THINGS ARE ALWAYS IN MOTION.

4
Close your eyes and see yourself aligning with source, blending into one.
Thank this constant focus upon you.

6
Feel and give thanks for the abundance of well-being all around.
For a full minute.

What 4 things would I like to turn over to the Universe to take care of for me today?

1._____
2._____
3._____
4._____

When you stop looking for the desired manifestation, you learn that the feeling grows and carries you to the destination.

Write what things you intend to do today and how you intend to feel as you accomplish these things.

1._____Feeling_____
2._____Feeling_____
3._____Feeling_____
4._____Feeling_____

I look forward to enjoying a productive and fun day.

Pick one of these emotions you would like to use
as today's intended feeling.
Ease, Relaxed, Comfort
Write this feeling here:_____
Now say to yourself...

1.
MY INTENTION IS TO REMIND MYSELF MANY TIMES TODAY...

FOCUSING ON THIS FEELING OF_____ IS MY REAL JOB FOR THE DAY.

2.
MY CURRENT CONDITIONS ARE IRRELEVANT BECAUSE...

I'M CREATING AN ENVIRONMENT THAT IS CAUSING THEM TO CHANGE.

3.
NO MORE SNAPSHOTS OF WHAT IS OR FEELING HELPLESS.

TODAY, I AM GOING TO USE THIS EMOTION AS MY BASE FEELING THAT WILL EFFECT FUTURE OUTCOMES.

Close your eyes again and reach for this intended feeing in
place of the feeling of current reality. Notice the softening
of your body as you aligning with source.

Write your chosen daily focused emotion reaching
for the feeling.

_____ _____ _____
_____ _____ _____
_____ _____ _____
_____ _____ _____

ASK YOURSELF MANY TIMES TODAY
"Is this the attracting vibration, I want the universe to respond to?"
If not, for the count of 10 long breaths in and
slowly letting them out.
Say and feel your chosen emotion in appreciation for the feeling.
It self-creates without any evidence needed.

Write 3 things you would be interested in seeing that just for fun but
you are not worried about when.

_____
_____
_____

Let the universe show you these things in playful and exciting ways.

A THOUGHT REACHES A COMBUSTION POINT AT 16 SECONDS.

Spend Your Vibrational Cash on one thing a day. If wanting a big ticket item slowly pay it off. This will make it more real for you.

VIBRATIONAL CASH

The longer you spend feeling like the recipient of this desire the closer you are in being a match to it.

A FULL 68 SECONDS ARE EQUIVALENT TO 2 MILLION MAN-HOURS.

Focus on how it feels to buy this desire and the satisfaction attached within having it. Write about that satisfaction.

Close your eyes again and reach for the first thing that pops into your mind. No matter what the price tag is, big and small creations are all the same. Learn to start treating them all equal.

VibrationalCash

Date

Pay To The Order Of

5,000.00

IN YOUR CURRENCY

LIVE THE EXPERIENCE IN THE NOW

FOR

Sign name here

ASK, BELIEVE,
RECEIVE

ASK

What are ready to take the vibrational journey to?
By asking for this desire it means you are creating a gap and your job is to close it.

BELIEVE/SOURCE

THE MINUTE YOU ASK, IT IS DONE VIBRATIONALLY COMPLETE AND 99.99% DONE PHYSICALLY

RECEIVE:

Create a momentum in belief by feeling it is yours for 20 second, snap shots at a time. Focusing only on feeling not image.

If you hold an emotion as the desire. You no longer are creating an impossibility. The shift from in the future having the desire becomes felt in the present moment, and you will notice the tension has left the solar plexus as you do this.
At this moment you are able to isolate the components of the desire even without having the desire. You become expectant, Being expectant is a very high frequency, and it is one step away from the manifestation to occur.

What do you feel ready to change in your life.
By asking you are now saying "I will deliberately start creating this climate to close the gap. I am aware of my part in how long the manifestation will take.

_____
_____
_____
_____
_____

Source has now become this vibrationally.
Your work is to create a mimicking or matching vibration.

Faith is created by reaching for the feeling and trusting the manifestation will follow.
Start now creating the feeling it is done by using small 20-second Virtual Realities while conjuring the emotions.
The idea is to preserve the focus that feels good longer, so you can match the frequency and enjoy the pleasures it provides in feelings.
Always leave the imagination
play through, if you feel anything but enjoyment.

POSITIVE ASPECTS

Appreciation is one of the highest vibrations you can use to shift how you are feeling.
It will build momentum fast and create an overall positive experience.
Even when you are in the worst of moods, if you focus on the parts that
you are appreciative for you will begin to start a new point of attraction.

I APPRECIATE YOU!
PERSON
NAME: *WHY?*

_____
_____
_____
_____
_____

I APPRECIATE THE
BEAUTY FOUND HERE.
PLACE: *WHY?*

_____
_____
_____
_____

I APPRECIATE THE
BEAUTY FOUND HERE.
PLACE: *WHY?*

_____
_____
_____
_____

I APPRECIATE YOU!
PERSON
NAME: *WHY?*

_____
_____
_____
_____

I APPRECIATE HAVING
ACCESS TO THIS.
THING: *WHY?*

_____
_____
_____
_____

WHAT I LOVE ABOUT
THE WEATHER: *WHY?*

_____
_____
_____

I APPRECIATE YOU!
PERSON
NAME: *WHY?*

_____
_____
_____

I APPRECIATE HAVING
ACCESS TO THIS.
THING: *WHY?*

_____
_____
_____

WHAT I LOVE ABOUT..
WHY?

_____
_____
_____

POSITIVE
ASPECTS

Focus on anything and everything. Saying "thank you"
Creates more things to be thankful for.

I AM THANKFUL FOR: *WHY?*

_____
_____
_____
_____
_____

I AM THANKFUL FOR: *WHY?*

_____
_____
_____
_____
_____

I AM THANKFUL FOR: *WHY?*

_____
_____
_____
_____
_____

I AM THANKFUL FOR: *WHY?*

_____
_____
_____
_____
_____

I AM THANKFUL FOR: *WHY?*

_____
_____
_____
_____
_____

I AM THANKFUL FOR: *WHY?*

_____
_____
_____
_____
_____

I AM THANKFUL FOR: *WHY?*

_____
_____
_____
_____
_____

I AM THANKFUL FOR: *WHY?*

_____
_____
_____
_____
_____

I AM THANKFUL FOR: *WHY?*

_____
_____
_____
_____
_____

FOODS

yum! WHAT MY BODY ENJOYED TODAY

_____
_____
_____
_____
_____
_____

WATER INTAKE

AM I HYDRATED?

GET PHYSICAL

WHAT MOVEMENT DID MY BODY ENJOY TODAY

_____
_____
_____
_____

MEDITATION

SPEND 15 MINS FOCUSING ON REPETITIVE SOUND. THE MORE BORING IT IS THE BETTER.

A TO Z

WRITE WORDS FROM A TO Z FEELING FOR THEM AS YOU WRITE THEM MAKE UP WORDS IF YOU CANT THINK OF ONE.

A_____ B_____ C_____ D_____

E_____ F_____ G_____ H_____

I_____ J_____ K_____ L_____

M_____ N_____ O_____ P_____

Q_____ R_____ S_____ T_____

U_____ V_____ W_____ X_____

Y_____ Z_____

Am I match ____
If I am feeling ease and comfort in this moment then I am.
I will sit in the feeling of satisfaction at focusing on these emotions right now.

1 SIT FOR ONE MINUTE BREATHING

Focus on holding a smile while taking in long and deep breaths in and slowly letting them out. Relax your body and feel the comfort of where you sit.

2 REMIND YOURSELF HOW IMPORTANT IT IS TO FEEL GOOD.

Today, nothing is more important then I feel good.

3
Write that here:

_____
_____
_____
_____
_____
_____
_____

5
NOTICE HOW THE SUN CAME UP AND THINGS ARE ALWAYS IN MOTION.

4
Close your eyes and see yourself aligning with source, blending into one.
Thank this constant focus upon you.

6
Feel and give thanks for the abundance of well-being all around.
For a full minute.

What 4 things would I like to turn over to the Universe to take care of for me today?

1._____
2._____
3._____
4._____

When you stop looking for the desired manifestation, you learn that the feeling grows and carries you to the destination.

Write what things you intend to do today and how you intend to feel as you accomplish these things.

1._____Feeling_____
2._____Feeling_____
3._____Feeling_____
4._____Feeling_____

I look forward to enjoying a productive and fun day.

Pick one of these emotions you would like to use
as today's intended feeling.
Ease, Relaxed, Comfort
Write this feeling here:_____
Now say to yourself...

**1.
MY INTENTION IS TO
REMIND MYSELF
MANY TIMES
TODAY...**

FOCUSING ON THIS
FEELING OF_____
IS MY REAL
JOB FOR THE DAY.

**2.
MY CURRENT
CONDITIONS ARE
IRRELEVANT
BECAUSE...**

I'M CREATING AN
ENVIRONMENT THAT
IS CAUSING THEM TO
CHANGE.

**3.
NO MORE SNAPSHOTS
OF WHAT IS
OR FEELING HELPLESS.**

TODAY, I AM GOING
TO USE THIS EMOTION
AS MY BASE FEELING
THAT WILL EFFECT
FUTURE OUTCOMES.

Close your eyes again and reach for this intended feeing in
place of the feeling of current reality. Notice the softening
of your body as you aligning with source.

Write your chosen daily focused emotion reaching
for the feeling.

_____ _____ _____
_____ _____ _____
_____ _____ _____
_____ _____ _____

ASK YOURSELF MANY TIMES TODAY
"Is this the attracting vibration, I want the universe to respond to?"
If not, for the count of 10 long breaths in and
slowly letting them out.
Say and feel your chosen emotion in appreciation for the feeling.
It self-creates without any evidence needed.

Write 3 things you would be interested in seeing that just for fun but
you are not worried about when.

_____
_____
_____

Let the universe show you these things in playful and exciting ways.

A THOUGHT REACHES A COMBUSTION POINT AT 16 SECONDS.

VIBRATIONAL
CASH

A FULL 68 SECONDS ARE EQUIVALENT TO 2 MILLION MAN-HOURS.

Spend Your Vibrational Cash on one thing a day. If wanting a big ticket item slowly pay it off. This will make it more real for you.

The longer you spend feeling like the recipient of this desire the closer you are in being a match to it.

Focus on how it feels to buy this desire and the satisfaction attached within having it. Write about that satisfaction.

Close your eyes again and reach for the first thing that pops into your mind. No matter what the price tag is, big and small creations are all the same. Learn to start treating them all equal.

VIBRATIONALCASH

DATE

PAY TO
THE ORDER OF

5,000.00

IN YOUR CURRENCY

LIVE THE EXPERIENCE IN THE NOW

FOR

SIGN NAME HERE

_____

_____

_____

_____

_____

_____

_____

_____

ASK, BELIEVE,
RECEIVE

ASK

What are ready to take the vibrational journey to?
By asking for this desire it means you are creating a gap and your job is to close it.

BELIEVE/SOURCE

THE MINUTE YOU ASK, IT IS DONE VIBRATIONALLY COMPLETE AND 99.99% DONE PHYSICALLY

RECEIVE:

Create a momentum in belief by feeling it is yours for 20 second, snap shots at a time. Focusing only on feeling not image.

If you hold an emotion as the desire. You no longer are creating an impossibility. The shift from in the future having the desire becomes felt in the present moment, and you will notice the tension has left the solar plexus as you do this.
At this moment you are able to isolate the components of the desire even without having the desire. You become expectant, Being expectant is a very high frequency, and it is one step away from the manifestation to occur.

What do you feel ready to change in your life.
By asking you are now saying "I will deliberately start creating this climate to close the gap.
I am aware of my part in how long the manifestation will take.

_____
_____
_____
_____
_____

Source has now become this vibrationally.
Your work is to create a mimicking or matching vibration.

Faith is created by reaching for the feeling and trusting the manifestation will follow.
Start now creating the feeling it is done by using small 20-second Virtual Realities while conjuring the emotions.
The idea is to preserve the focus that feels good longer, so you can match the frequency and enjoy the pleasures it provides in feelings.
Always leave the imagination play through, if you feel anything but enjoyment.

POSITIVE ASPECTS

Appreciation is one of the highest vibrations you can use to shift how you are feeling.
It will build momentum fast and create an overall positive experience.
Even when you are in the worst of moods, if you focus on the parts that
you are appreciative for you will begin to start a new point of attraction.

I APPRECIATE YOU!
PERSON
NAME: *WHY?*

_____
_____
_____
_____
_____

I APPRECIATE THE
BEAUTY FOUND HERE.
PLACE: *WHY?*

_____
_____
_____
_____
_____

I APPRECIATE THE
BEAUTY FOUND HERE.
PLACE: *WHY?*

_____
_____
_____
_____
_____

I APPRECIATE YOU!
PERSON
NAME: *WHY?*

_____
_____
_____
_____
_____

I APPRECIATE HAVING
ACCESS TO THIS.
THING: *WHY?*

_____
_____
_____
_____
_____

WHAT I LOVE ABOUT
THE WEATHER: *WHY?*

_____
_____
_____
_____
_____

I APPRECIATE YOU!
PERSON
NAME: *WHY?*

_____
_____
_____
_____

I APPRECIATE HAVING
ACCESS TO THIS.
THING: *WHY?*

_____
_____
_____
_____

WHAT I LOVE ABOUT..

                         WHY?

_____
_____
_____
_____

POSITIVE
ASPECTS

Focus on anything and everything. Saying "thank you"
Creates more things to be thankful for.

I AM THANKFUL FOR: *WHY?*

_____
_____
_____
_____
_____

I AM THANKFUL FOR: *WHY?*

_____
_____
_____
_____
_____

I AM THANKFUL FOR: *WHY?*

_____
_____
_____
_____
_____

I AM THANKFUL FOR: *WHY?*

_____
_____
_____
_____
_____

I AM THANKFUL FOR: *WHY?*

_____
_____
_____
_____
_____

I AM THANKFUL FOR: *WHY?*

_____
_____
_____
_____
_____

I AM THANKFUL FOR: *WHY?*

_____
_____
_____
_____

I AM THANKFUL FOR: *WHY?*

_____
_____
_____
_____

I AM THANKFUL FOR: *WHY?*

_____
_____
_____
_____

FOODS
yum! WHAT MY BODY ENJOYED TODAY

_____

_____

_____

_____

_____

_____

WATER INTAKE
AM I HYDRATED?

GET PHYSICAL
WHAT MOVEMENT DID MY BODY ENJOY TODAY

_____

_____

_____

_____

MEDITATION

SPEND 15 MINS FOCUSING ON REPETITIVE SOUND. THE MORE BORING IT IS THE BETTER.

A TO Z

WRITE WORDS FROM A TO Z FEELING FOR THEM AS YOU WRITE THEM MAKE UP WORDS IF YOU CANT THINK OF ONE.

A_____ B_____ C_____ D_____

E_____ F_____ G_____ H_____

I_____ J_____ K_____ L_____

M_____ N_____ O_____ P_____

Q_____ R_____ S_____ T_____

U_____ V_____ W_____ X_____

Y_____ Z_____

Am I match ____
If I am feeling ease and comfort in this moment then I am.
I will sit in the feeling of satisfaction at focusing on these emotions right now.